FLYING BOATS

THE J-CLASS YACHTS OF AVIATION

FLYING BOATS

THE J-CLASS YACHTS OF AVIATION

Written and Illustrated by

IAN MARSHALL

HOWELL PRESS

Designed by Carolyn Weary Brandt
Edited by James R. Knowles

Library of Congress Cataloging-in-Publication Data

Marshall, Ian (Ian H.)
    Flying boats : the J-class yachts of aviation / Ian Marshall.
        p. cm.
    Includes bibliographical references and index.
    ISBN 1-57427-121-0 (hardcover)
    1. Seaplanes. 2. Airplanes in art. I. Title.

  TL684.M37 2002
  629.133'347—dc21

                                                              2001059442

ISBN 1-57427-121-0

Printed in Singapore

Published by Howell Press
1713-2D Allied Lane
Charlottesville, VA 22903
(434) 977-4006
www.howellpress.com

First Printing 2002

André Priester, chief engineer of Pan American Airways during the flying boat era, was renowned and respected throughout the company. It was his custom to make his own Christmas card each year, and employees would treasure these cards when they received them. Above is a reproduction of the card for Christmas 1938, which was sent to John Leslie, manager of the Pacific Division of PAA. It is reproduced by kind permission of his children.

Dedicated to my wife

Jean Carol MacCarthy Marshall

In memory of a flight in an East African Airways

de Havilland DH 89 Dragon Rapide from Entebbe to Bukoba

When we were weighed

In the 1920s, car makers used to embellish their radiator filler caps, or the hoods that covered them, with mascots. One practical company used a small glass thermometer, several had eagles, one used a jaguar and one a tall, flowing figure suggestive of the Winged Victory of Samothrace. Another make used the bold profile and feathered head-dress of a native of Michigan. The Hispano-Suiza sported an elegant stork in flight, but best of all was Armstrong-Siddeley. The stately motorcars built by this British company carried on their bonnet the miniature silver figure of an Egyptian sphinx. Armstrongs, like Hispanos, were also in the business of making aero engines, and they provided Imperial Airways with a fleet of limousines with which to convey their passengers in suitable manner from central London to Croydon Airport.

Blohm & Voss BV 222. 150 ft wingspan, range 2,100 miles. First flew in 1940, fourteen were used by the Luftwaffe.

CONTENTS

List of Paintings...............................8

Acknowledgments...........................10

Overview...13

Plates...30

Bibliography.................................134

Index...135

LIST OF PAINTINGS

Frontispiece. Martin M-130 *China Clipper*, Shadows on the Sand..................2

Plate 1. NC-4 at Horta, in the Azores Islands, during the first Atlantic crossing by air, 1919..................31

Plate 2. Curtiss F5-L at the Casa Marina Hotel, Key West, 1922..................33

Plate 3. Short Singapore 1 of Sir Alan Cobham at Port Bell, Uganda, 1927....35

Plate 4. Short S 8 Calcutta alighting at Corfu, 1929..................37

Plate 5. Consolidated Commodore of NYRBA over Rio de Janeiro, 1930..........39

Plate 6. Short S 17 Kent *Scipio* coming in to alight at Alexandria, 1931..........41

Plate 7. Sikorsky S-40 *Caribbean Clipper* at Panama City, 1931..................43

Plate 8. Latécoère 300 *Croix du Sud* alighting at Natal, Brazil, 1934..............45

Plate 9. Consolidated Commodore shortly before alighting at Nassau, Bahama Islands, 1934..................47

Plate 10. Sikorsky S-42, S-38, and S-40 flying boats at Dinner Key, Miami, 1935..................49

Plate 11. Bréguet 530 Saigon *Algérie* over the coast of North Africa, 1935.......51

Plate 12. Sikorsky S-38 *Carnauba* over the Amazon forest in Brazil, 1935.......53

Plate 13. Martin M-130 *China Clipper* at Wake Island, 1935..................55

Plate 14. Blériot 5190 *Santos Dumont* at Rio de Janeiro, 1935..................57

Plate 15. Sikorsky S-42A *Jamaica Clipper*, background Pão de Açúcar, Rio de Janeiro, 1936..................59

Plate 16. Short S 17 Kents and Short S 8 Calcuttas moored off Hythe in Southampton Water, 1936..................61

Plate 17. Sikorsky S-43s of Panair do Brasil at Rio de Janeiro, 1936...............63

Plate 18. Short S 23 "Empire" flying boat taking off at Rod-El-Farag, Cairo, 1936..................65

Plate 19. Martin M-130 *Hawaiian Clipper* over the incomplete Golden Gate Bridge, San Francisco, 1936..................67

Plate 20. Sikorsky S-42B *Samoan Clipper* at Pago Pago, American Samoa, 1937..................69

Plate 21. Short S 23 "Empire" boat *Capella* just at splash-down on Lake Naivasha, Kenya, 1937..................71

Plate 22. Dornier Do 18 flying boat and Blohm & Voss Ha 139 floatplane at Horta, Azores, 1937..................73

Plate 23. Dornier Do J II Wal being catapulted from ss *Westfallen*, with Dornier Do 26 overhead, 1938..................75

Plate 24. Short-Mayo S 20 *Mercury* floatplane immediately after disengagement from Short S 21 *Maia* flying boat, 1938..................77

Plate 25. Sikorsky S-42A *Antilles Clipper* landing at Dinner Key, Miami, 1938..................79

Plate 26. Short S 23 "Empire" boat *Coriolanus* from the rest house verandah at Koepang, Timor, 1938..................81

Plate 27. Short S 23 "Empire" boat *Calypso* at Mombasa, Kenya, 1938..........83

Plate 28. Sikorsky S-42B *Bermuda Clipper* landing on the Great Sound, Bermuda, 1939..................85

Plate 29. Martin M-130 *Philippine Clipper* at Treasure Island Marine Air Terminal, San Francisco Bay, 1939..................87

Plate 30. Short S 23 "Empire" boat *Cassiopeia* boarding passengers at Luxor, 1939..................89

Plate 31. Boeing B-314 *Honolulu Clipper* at Treasure Island, San Francisco Bay, 1939.................91

Plate 32. Consolidated PBY-2 *Guba* at Diego Garcia in the Chagos Archipelago, with the cruiser HMS *Manchester*, 1939.................93

Plate 33. Short S 23 "Empire" boat *Ceres* boarding passengers at Laropi on the Albert Nile, Uganda, 1939.................95

Plate 34. Boeing B-314 *Dixie Clipper* loading passengers at Port Washington, Long Island, New York, 1939.................97

Plate 35. Latécoère 522 *Ville de Saint Pierre* overflying SS *Normandie*, July 30, 1939.................99

Plate 36. Short S 30 "Empire" boat *Cabot* at Berth 108, Southampton, 1939.................101

Plate 37. Boeing B-314 taking off from Bowery Bay, off New York's La Guardia Marine Air Terminal, 1940.................103

Plate 38. Boeing B-314 *Atlantic Clipper* at moorings in the Tagus River, opposite Lisbon waterfront, 1940.................105

Plate 39. Foynes, on the Shannon River, Ireland, 1941. Two Boeing B-314s, one Short S 23, and one Short Sunderland flying boat at moorings.........107

Plate 40. Sikorsky VS-44A *Excalibur*, 1942.................109

Plate 41. Consolidated PBY-5A "Black Cat," Guadalcanal, 1943.................111

Plate 42. Short S 25 Sunderland III taxiing for takeoff from the Cattewater, RAF Mount Batten, Plymouth, 1943.................113

Plate 43. Boeing B-314 alighting at Bathurst, the Gambia, with President Roosevelt on board, 1943.................115

Plate 44. Short S 25 Hythe *Himalaya* overflying the Pyramids of Gizeh, Cairo, 1946.................117

Plate 45. Latécoère 631 at Martinique, 1947.................119

Plate 46. Latécoère 631 flying over Fort-de-France, Martinique, 1947.................121

Plate 47. Short S 45 Solent *Salisbury* overflying the Victoria Falls before landing on the Zambezi River, 1949.................123

Plate 48. Short S 45 Solent Mk IV *Aotearoa* landing at Waitemata Harbour, Auckland, 1950.................125

Plate 49. Short S 45 Solent II *Somerset* at Cape Maclear, Lake Nyasa, November 1950.................127

Plate 50. Saunders-Roe SR 45 Princess flying boats near Calshot Castle, Southampton Water, 1952.................129

Plate 51. Grumman G-38 Goose of Antilles Airboats at Saint Thomas, 1973.................131

Plate 52. Grumman G-73 Turbo Mallard of Virgin Islands Seaplane Shuttle at Saint Thomas, 1986.................133

Imperial Airways terminal in Buckingham Palace Road, London

ACKNOWLEDGMENTS

Many people have contributed their knowledge and their tales about flying boats. I want to thank particularly Dann and Sherry Lewis and George Hambleton for the inspiration, Peter Leslie and other members of his family for their enthusiasm and for so kindly putting at my disposal their father's papers and their own insights, and Louie Howland for giving me an apt subtitle. I am specially grateful to R. E. G. Davies, Curator of Air Transport at the National Air and Space Museum, Smithsonian Institution, for his extraordinarily generous offer to cast an eagle eye over my text, and for contributing numerous details of fact and tact, as well as some personal gems.

Others who have most kindly devoted time and attention include Paul A. Roitsch, Kathleen M. Clair, Robert P. Scarsdale, John Borger, and Fyfe Symington of the Pan American Airways Historical Foundation; Régis Dognin, Peter Johnson, Harold Pember, Harold Haleva, Phil Spalla and a host of colleagues at Sikorsky Aircraft Corporation; David A. Fink of Pan American Airways; Lord Marshall and Fred Walker of British Airways; Margaret O'Shaughnessy of the Flying Boat Museum at Foynes; flying boat aficionado Dave Straub; John Spenceley, onetime PAA Station Manager; and Kinnear Macdonald, who provided some particularly interesting and useful technical advice. I am greatly indebted to the authors of many books listed in the bibliography, and especially to Gerald Durrell for his breathtaking description of watching a flying boat land at Corfu, which occurs in *My Family and Other Animals*. Thank you, Tom Pilgram, for drawing my attention to this passage. Heartfelt thanks to my wife, Jean, for putting up with this and for all the keyboard stuff, once again.

Sikorsky S–38

FLYING BOATS

Latécoère 581

FLYING BOATS

The J-Class Yachts of Aviation

André Priester, chief engineer of Pan American Airways, had a phrase for it: "A flying boat is an airplane that carries its landing field on its bottom."

So, indeed, does a goose. The flying boats had an endearing quality, a little ungainly, perhaps, but dignified. Some would say they were distinctly zoomorphic. One of Pan Am's most famous pilots, Marius Lodeesen, differs from this view. He said of the Sikorsky S-40: "She could fly, after a fashion. She took to the air with the profundity of a dowager rising from the sofa at a *soirée chez Duchesse de Guermantes.*"

Flying boats had a boat-like hull on the underside, and most of them were provided with small wingtip floats to keep them balanced while on the water. Floatplanes, on the other hand, were generally smaller, landplane types, fitted with large floats or pontoons in place of wheels. The term seaplane usually applied to the latter, although it is sometimes used now to encompass all waterborne aircraft.

They were proper boats, with anchors and little retractable bollards in the bow. They carried inflatable dinghies, and once they were on the water they hoisted the national ensign. Flying boat captains wore naval uniforms and had to pass examinations in seamanship. They knew all about tide tables and navigation marks, they could "shoot the stars" with a sextant, they could tell an isobar from an isotherm, and they had to be able to pick up a mooring under a cross wind in a busy harbor. The British gave their planes the prefix RMA, for Royal Mail Aircraft, and Pan Am called theirs Clippers.

In the early 1930s, airfields were rare. Throughout the most thickly settled parts of the United States and Europe you could find a few, but practically all of them were just grass strips. Some, like London's Croydon, were notorious for being built on the crest of a gentle hill: you couldn't even see if there was an aircraft at the other end of the runway. The first paved runway in Europe was not laid down until 1936, at Stockholm. Before that, in spring, it was commonplace for pilots to find themselves bogged down in mud.

To fly abroad, you had to think carefully about stepping-stones along the way. It wasn't enough for airlines to obtain a permit to land; they also had to contemplate constructing their own landing fields to make it possible. With aircraft of limited range, such fields could not be far apart, so on a new route, in a foreign country, the difficulties were formidable.

There was precedent for going by sea. International law had long established the right of ships to ply the oceans, and ships were free to enter foreign ports subject only to customs duties on landed goods. On the other hand, several countries were being very difficult about permission to overfly, and already in 1930 landing rights, or traffic rights, were beginning to become a subject of contention. This has not changed.

Airplanes of those days were likely to find that they had to land inadvertently. The internal combustion engine couldn't compare with steam for reliability.

Radio direction-finding beacons existed only along the principal US mail routes and they were of limited range. Wireless was unreliable, and weather forecasting was in its infancy. Put these factors together and you could easily lose your way. The most important new instruments available to a pilot were the Sperry gyro automatic horizon and the turn and bank indicator, but these were of little help to navigation.

A landplane, flying blind over uncertain territory, risked flying into a hill or having to come down to earth in a tropical jungle. A flying boat, on the other hand, could hug the coastline or follow a broad river, secure in the knowledge that it would always be in reach of water on which to alight. When it came to setting out across the open sea, many people found it more comforting to do so in a boat, of sorts.

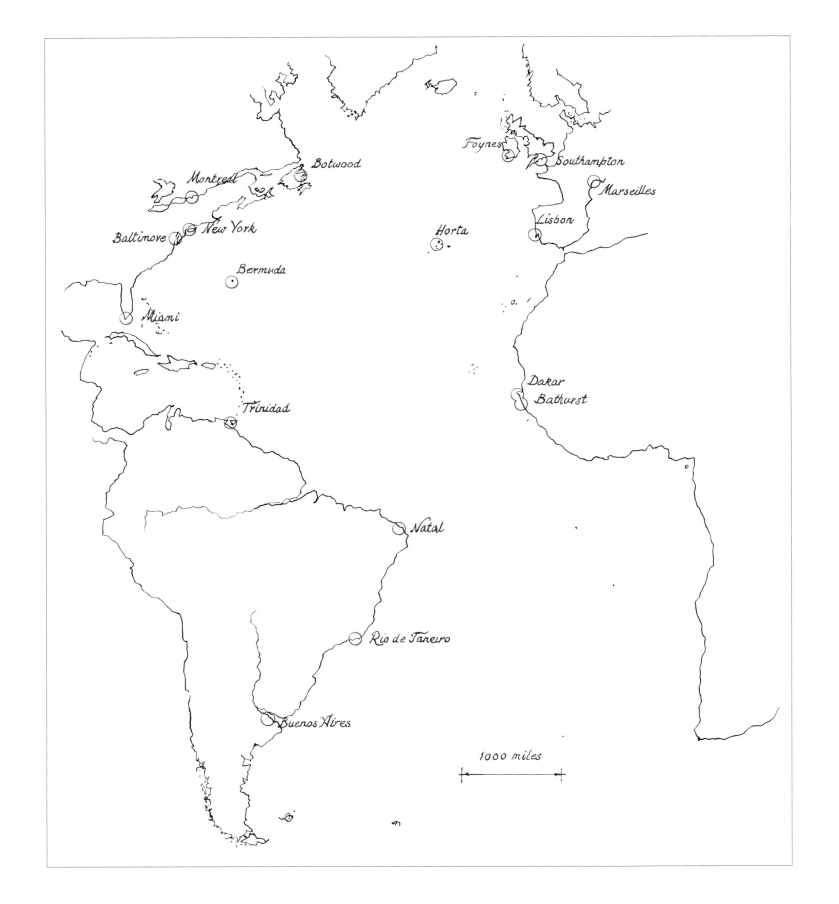

Foynes
Southampton
Botwood
Montreal
Marseilles
New York
Lisbon
Baltimore
Horta
Bermuda
Miami
Trinidad
Dakar
Bathurst
Natal
Rio de Janeiro
Buenos Aires

1000 miles

In 1930, one fledgling airline was already heavily into flying boats. It was called Pan American Airways. The corporation was then just over two years old, and showing signs of a precocious and acquisitive personality. It flew out of Miami to a network of destinations around the Caribbean, to Cuba, Puerto Rico, Venezuela, Colombia, Central America, and Mexico. On these routes, it operated thirty S-38 flying boats. These spindly little Sikorsky amphibians were equipped with wheels, which allowed them to alight on land or water. They had two engines and seats for eight passengers. In August 1930, Pan American outwitted and bought out a company called the New York, Rio, and Buenos Aires Line (NYRBA). NYRBA employed eleven Consolidated Commodores on its long-distance service down the eastern seaboard of South America, and these stately antecedents of the famous wartime PBY Catalina, together with the lucrative airmail route which they plied, were added to the Pan American system. When the company needed planes with longer range to bridge the Caribbean, it turned to Sikorsky to supply a larger version of the S-38. The new type, the S-40, had four engines and could carry thirty-eight passengers over a distance half as far again as its predecessor. Three of these boats were placed in service in 1931–32.

Increased size, speed, and range led to aircraft of greater weight and higher landing speed. For a flying boat this was not a problem. The heavier boat simply displaced more water; landing strips cost nothing to build. For a landplane, increased weight meant more punch on impact, and the outcome was that runways needed to be built with much more substantial foundations as well as greater length. It also meant that a landplane's undercarriage became a serious encumbrance, absorbing as much as five percent of the tare weight.

Alighting on water, on the other hand, had its own drawbacks. The hull had to be broad and strong enough to withstand the heavy splash; it had to be reasonably seaworthy to cope with choppy conditions; and it had to be skillfully designed to provide directional stability during takeoff and landing. Flying boats were apt to heel over in a wind—or if they were turned in the water too abruptly—whereupon they could dunk an engine or submerge a wing. They therefore needed wingtip floats, or water-level stabilizers called spon-

sons. Some types of boats were inclined to porpoise, that is to pitch lengthwise if landed injudiciously.

Leaving the water also had its difficulties. Drag defied efforts to reach takeoff speed, and experienced flying boat passengers learned surreptitiously to time the takeoff run. Yacht designers helped to develop hull forms incorporating a step to allow the rear part to break out of the water first. During the last part of the run, the hull would plane largely out of the water, thereby allowing the aircraft to continue accelerating and achieve the critical speed. Nevertheless, flying boats were often defeated by too rough conditions, or because they had trouble breaking the surface tension when trying to take to the air from a surface which was completely unruffled (pilots would taxi the plane around to cause waves, or a speedboat would be sent to do the job for them). Hydrodynamic design, which called for broad, flared hulls with pronounced chines and steps, was at odds with aerodynamic requirements. Another difficulty was keeping a water runway clear: even an insignificant piece of flotsam drifting into the path of a flying boat could present a major hazard.

I was told of one Boeing 314 which was disabled for ten days in the River Gambia in West Africa during the Second World War. Replacement parts for the faulty engine were flown in; the station manager joined with mechanics and learned how to tension cylinder-head nuts correctly, working in steamy heat. Finally the engines were tested. Full power was achieved: all systems were working satisfactorily, and the Clipper was loaded up and taxied out for takeoff. At full throttle she couldn't be coaxed to takeoff speed. Three times the captain tried, but all in vain. Returning to the dock, my friend leaned over to tie a mooring line. He happened to glance under the water, and there he noticed barnacles and seaweed. The underside of the hull, squatting in tropical water, had accumulated a wig of sea growth.

Refueling, maintenance, and handling baggage were all a great deal more difficult to manage on the water. Today's volumes of air traffic could never have been handled at moorings or docks. On the other hand, the paucity of infrastructure at flying boat stops made it quite easy to vary their routes.

While the airlines managed to overcome many of these early difficulties, the factor that would have sunk the flying boats sooner or later was corrosion. Spray, particularly saltwater spray, thrown up into props and ingested by engines, was a serious problem. The ships were built with deep hulls to minimize this, but it reduced their aerodynamic efficiency. More subtly, saltwater gently permeated the riveted aluminum skin, going to work on the unseen structure within a hull.

The short but debonair career of the flying boats was brought to an end when airfields became available. The war years saw the construction of airstrips for military use in every part of the world, most of them with hard runways. Cities rushed to create terminal facilities. Now it was not up to the airlines to consider the cost; they were positively courted by cities to come their way.

In the changed circumstances, competing airlines went for airplanes with the best combination of speed, range, economy, and load-carrying performance. The cost of building longer runways with heavily reinforced concrete foundations, the displacement of houses, the inexorable spread of aircraft noise and pollution—all were now matters for someone else to cope with. Between 1939 and 1945 the terms of the operating cost equation had been completely changed.

Crossing the Atlantic by Air

The first aircraft to cross the Atlantic was a flying boat. Soon after the guns fell silent at the end of the agony known as the Great War, the US Navy determined to be first to fly the ocean. Before the fleet was demobilized, no less than sixty-eight destroyers supported by five battleships were stationed in a line across the sea, and in May 1919, three Navy Curtiss flying boats set off in company to cross from Long Island, via Newfoundland, the Azores Islands, and Lisbon, to Plymouth in the south of England. One of them, NC-4, made it. After fifteen days en route and fifty-four hours in the air, Lt. Commander Read and his crew achieved the goal of First Across.

Their record stood unchallenged for eighteen days. Less than three weeks later, two British fliers, Alcock and Brown, departed rather shakily from a cow pasture in Newfoundland with the intention of flying clear across in one leap.

They piloted a Vickers Vimy landplane, a wartime bomber that had been built for raiding Berlin. They had some hair-raising experiences, but—by the skin of their teeth—they, too, succeeded in landing safely on the other side. They made landfall close to where they intended, but with no profusion of landing fields to choose from in the west of Ireland, they had the misfortune to select a pasture that turned out to be more like a bog. Their flight time was sixteen hours.

Two weeks later, the airship R34 left Scotland and arrived unannounced over New York after 108 hours in the air. Three days later the ship diffidently returned in a period of seventy-five hours; this was the first east-west crossing, and it was also the first round trip.

During the twenty years between 1919 and the outbreak of the Second World War, there were a great many attempts to fly the Atlantic. Numerous efforts were ill-conceived and ill-equipped, and many came to grief. A handful of others made the crossing via Iceland or via South America before 1927, but Charles Lindbergh's achievement in that year stands out for the careful, deliberate planning which he devoted to the enterprise. He had the meticulous and scientific approach of an engineer, he had an airplane built to his own specifications, he paid respect to the shortcomings of others, and he was a superb pilot.

Lindbergh flew nonstop from New York to Paris, 3,600 miles, compared to Alcock and Brown's 2,000 miles across the shortest route.

US National Ensign

His airplane had much improved instrumentation compared to those of 1919. Lindbergh had better luck with the weather than Alcock and Brown, but he boldly took to the air alone, and his success was a personal triumph. Numerous adventurers followed suit. By 1938, forty-five successful crossings had been achieved, but there was a long list of failures.

The North Atlantic air route had special attractions, and it also had special difficulties. The importance of this route was that it connected what were then the world's two great centers of commerce. The potential traffic, in passengers, mails, and valuable freight, was by far the greatest on earth.

Difficulties included not just distance, but geography and climate.

Several routes were possible: the northern via Labrador, Greenland, Iceland and possibly the Faroe Islands; the direct route via Newfoundland and Ireland; and the southern via Bermuda, the Azores, and Lisbon.

Commercial service called for consistency, that is, year-round operations adhering to a timetable, and it required, of course, the capacity to carry sufficient payload in addition to the weight of aircraft, crew, and necessary fuel. Prevailing winds out of the west rendered westbound crossings much more arduous. Winter storms made the northern and direct routes seasonally hazardous; visibility, and therefore navigation, was often impaired, and ice made winter flying boat landings unwise in Newfoundland, Nova Scotia, and even in Long Island Sound. A final twist was that the Azores Islands, an essential stepping-stone on the southern route, harbored no sheltered stretch of water. Massive Atlantic swells, which impinged even within the breakwater which forms a roadstead at Horta, would infuriatingly prevent landings or takeoffs for up to two weeks at a time. No airports existed there, or in Bermuda, until they were created during the war.

Pan American Clippers

The first type of airplane with the range, speed, and load-carrying capacity to operate commercially across the Atlantic was Pan American's Boeing 314 flying boat of 1939.

Through the summer months from 1937 to 1939 there were many experiments and so-called proving flights. In addition to the United States, Great Britain, France, and Germany were all busily preparing transatlantic operations. In September 1939, however, Adolf Hitler started the Second World War, and the Europeans stopped all work abruptly.

When the Boeing Clippers went into service that summer, they placed America in the forefront of civil aviation. Pan American's achievement presaged an era. Since 1945, worldwide airlines have used American equipment almost exclusively. There is a remarkably close parallel with the situation one hundred years earlier, when the technology of iron steamships, built in British yards, swept the shipping world and dominated trade routes until long after the turn of the nineteenth century.

Success was due, in the first place, to the design and construction of the

aircraft. It is very revealing to observe the contrast in methods of procurement on opposite sides of the ocean. But that is only part of the picture. Equally important was Pan American's broad scope of experience in long-distance passenger flying operations, its record of innovation, and its cautious, deliberate approach to solving safety problems. Pan American's experience of operating over the great wastes of the Pacific during the years 1935-39 put it way in advance of British, French, Dutch, or German aviation at that time. It was the scientific approach to flight planning—the development of ocean navigation, including construction of long-range radio direction finding beacons, remote weather forecasting, systematic training and discipline of crews, with careful attention to maintenance and routine procedures—that made Pan American the leader in air transportation.

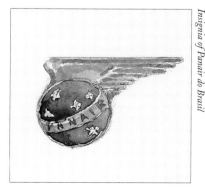

The airline played the principal part in promoting the development of aircraft to suit its operations. In particular, the company's ambitious and impatient president, Juan Trippe, prodded, challenged, and provoked manufacturers into creating airliners with capabilities in excess of what they themselves regarded as practicable. On one occasion he even placed an order to manufacture

Pan Am's globe in the Marine Air Terminal at Dinner Key

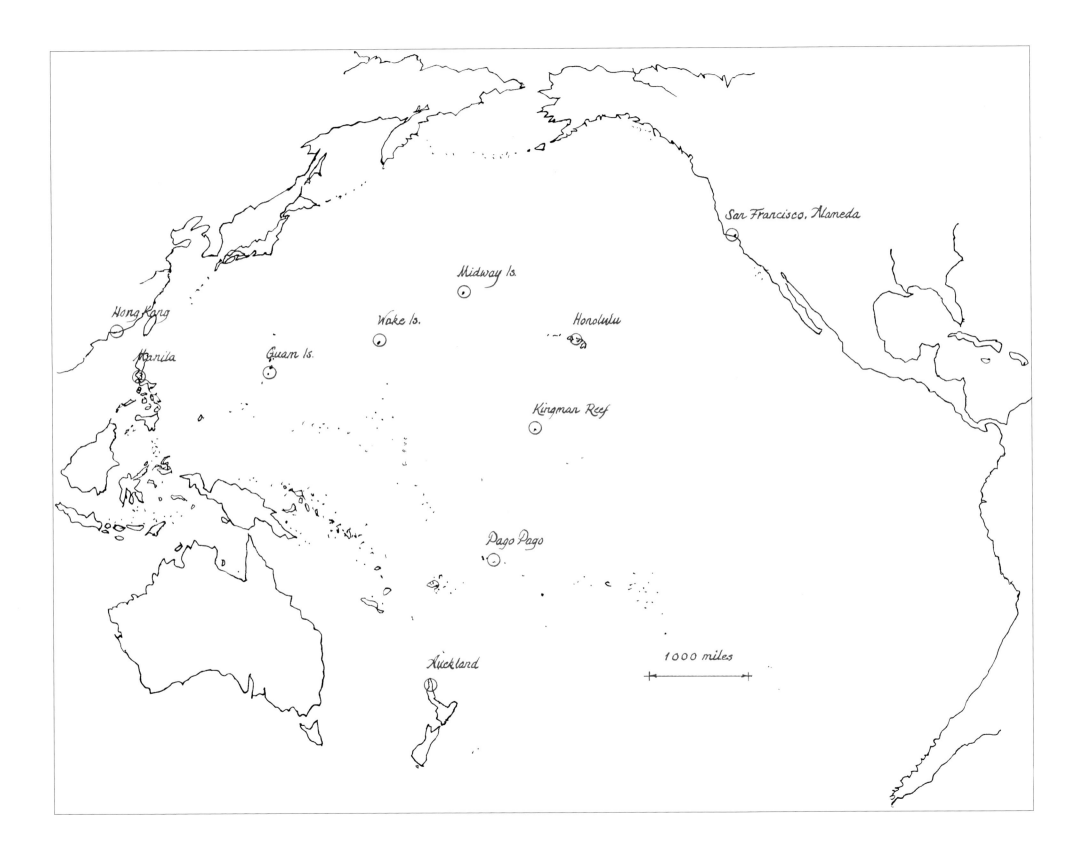

San Francisco, Alameda

Midway Is.

Hong Kong

Wake Is.

Honolulu

Manila

Guam Is.

Kingman Reef

Pago Pago

Auckland

1000 miles

116 aero engines—this was in the age of the big jets—to twist the arms of Boeing, Lockheed, and Douglas to design and build commensurate aircraft. The commercial risk was breathtaking, but it was a deliberate, calculated speculation.

Another intriguing detail of Pan American's history is the characteristic top deck hump worn by all Boeing 747s. That is the outcome of the airline's cautious assessment during the design stage that the type might be superseded for passenger use, in which case it could become desirable to transform the main deck of the 747 to all-cargo configuration with front-end loading. Such an airplane has, indeed, materialized.

Trippe's team was impressive. Pan American's chief engineer from the very early days of the company was the redoubtable André Priester, who came from the Netherlands. He was held in great respect by colleagues and regarded with trepidation by manufacturers. Priester was described as dedicated, exacting to the point of pedantic, and insistent upon perfection. He was equally concerned with what today would be termed "career development" among the staff; he introduced the policy of "multiple crew," each member being trained in more than one job, and he believed in duplication of mechanical systems. A Pan American crew of seven might include five qualified pilots.

Trippe also recruited the national hero, Charles Lindbergh, in the early days of the airline. His association with the company was a tremendous asset

Imperial Airways and BOAC "Speedbird"

in public relations, and he was retained as technical adviser well into the era of the 747, always encouraging others to search beyond what was currently possible. Hugo Leuteritz, the radio engineer from RCA who shared the prudent, orderly methods of Priester, was chiefly responsible for inventing a navigation system to make transoceanic flying practicable. There were, of course, many great pilots, led by Ed Musick, compact and meticulous, who "flew like the devil and never said much."

Pan American bred dedicated company men such as John Leslie, a far-sighted engineer, who created a well-oiled organization in one hemisphere after the other. Igor Sikorsky, though not in the team, should also be recognized, for he was the one who first built an airplane to meet the specific needs of the

airline. A Russian émigré, he was founder and chief designer of the renowned Sikorsky aircraft company which is now known worldwide for its helicopters. John Leslie described him as one of the most courteous, considerate, and modest gentlemen who ever lived. Leslie seemed to have a sort of intrinsic feel for what it took to create a capable organization, complementing Lindbergh's feel for what was needed in the air.

By contrast, the British airline engaged in overseas flying, which until 1940 was called Imperial Airways, muddled along with a mixture of motives, part strictly commercial and part public policy. There was a gulf between the operating company, which was responsible to its shareholders for returning a profit, and the aircraft manufacturers, whose products were specified and paid for partly by the Air Ministry.

Routes and choice of aircraft were determined largely by the government, but subsidies were meager. The system of payment for carriage of mails bore no comparison to the enterprising sponsorship of new routes which was the essence of the handsome long-term contracts offered by the US Postal Service.

Imperial Airways was a pioneer of international air travel, but it found itself struggling to make a living. One account describes how the company would cash a check in central London on a Friday to pay employees, trusting that the revenue from weekend flights to Paris would be deposited before the check arrived for clearance at the bank's branch in Croydon on Monday. It also operated the world's longest air route, 13,000 miles, from Croydon to Brisbane, Australia.

Public policy was guided by such objectives as promoting a broad geographical spread of employment, sharing-out contracts among various manufacturers, and strengthening the ties of empire by providing service to far-flung and

British Civil Air Ensign

sometimes quite insignificant destinations. The directors of Imperial Airways never remotely conceived the pot of gold that was to be won by generating enough traffic, particularly the enormous potential on the North Atlantic route.

Between the wars, America's best asset was its lead in aero engines. The big radials, Wright Cyclones and Pratt and Whitney Wasps and Hornets, gave the impetus. Again and again, European aircraft designs were crippled by engines that failed to come up to expectations. Power and economy were the key to speed, range, and load-carrying ability, but for ocean crossings reliability was what concentrated the mind. Reciprocating internal-combustion engines are complicated machines, containing hundreds of moving parts. The number of hours of flying time available between overhauls was a matter of vital commercial importance. Propellers were always a source of trouble. The development of controllable-pitch, and then of automatically variable-pitch propellers—so-called "constant-speed" propellers—made an important contribution to economy. The latter were first used on the S-42.

During the 1940s, it became evident that British aero engines were by then second to none in technical progress, notably the Rolls-Royce Merlin and Napier Sabre liquid-cooled in-line engines and the Bristol Hercules and Centaurus radials. During the same decade, British firms, parallel with German ones, were at the cutting edge in development of gas turbines.

The great age of passenger flying started only after 1958, with the availability of gas turbine propulsion. Rotary turbine engines are intrinsically simpler and far more dependable than piston engines, and they can go for far longer between overhauls. They transformed the reliability and the economics of airline operation, just as the vertical triple-expansion steam engine transformed the shipping trade after 1870.

In 1932, Pan American placed an order for the Sikorsky S-42. It made a giant stride forward in design. To meet the demand for a long-range aircraft,

Sikorsky believed in having a high wing-loading and extendable flaps. In plan, the wing was narrow in relation to the span, which reduced drag. Load-carrying capacity increases with the square of wind velocity across the wing, but takeoff and landing present difficulties. By using a thin and narrow high-speed wing, performance in flight was improved, and by using flaps to extend and depress the trailing edge, additional lift could be provided at lower speeds for landing and takeoff. The S-42's wings supported thirty pounds per square foot, twice the weight of previous types. Her load-to-tare weight ratio was an unprecedented 42 : 58; in

other words, the empty plane weighed little more than what she could carry by way of crew, fuel, and payload. Pilots said she landed "like a bear."

To a greater extent than previous designs, the structure depended on stressed skin for rigidity, rather than spars and framing. Drag was reduced by flush riveting, and by attention to the study of airflow over engine cowlings and wing fillets. Instrumentation was improved to enhance pilots' control over engine settings for maximum economy, and a radio direction finding loop was mounted above the cabin. Most of these features became standard practice in aircraft design thereafter.

The S-42s, or Betsys, as they were affectionately called, went into service first on flights throughout the Caribbean and down the east coast of South America. Ten were delivered to Pan American between 1934 and 1937, later models having increased power and range. They could carry up to thirty-two passengers over a distance of 1,200 miles, but were regularly employed over greater ranges with reduced capacity, culminating in Pacific and Atlantic proving flights of up to twice that distance without payload. To illustrate the delicate nature of the equation between speed, range, and payload, it was calculated that an S-42 consumed fuel equal to the weight of one passenger every fifteen minutes.

Engines could be stressed at full power for a limited period to get airborne with a full load of fuel in addition to payload, but they couldn't be run this way continuously. Pan American used extensive trials on new airplanes to determine gas consumption at different air speeds, altitudes, and gross weights. In daily service they would meet tailwinds, turbulence, headwinds, and freak storm conditions, as well as still air. Efficiency and safety depended on a carefully prepared flight plan and constant attention to changing conditions as the fuel load was depleted. Leslie said of the long-distance Pacific routes, "We didn't want to open them to passengers until we felt absolutely confident in our own minds that we had mastered the rudiments of the art."

A year after the first S-42, the larger Martin M-130 was delivered. There were only three of these flying boats, but though somewhat slower, they were capable of greater range. Their performance was just equal to carrying a handful of passengers over the longest sector of the Pacific routes, the 2,400-mile stretch between San Francisco and Honolulu. It took twenty hours in the air. So, in November 1935, Pan American inaugurated the first Pacific airmail service, with M-130s operating through Hawaii and via the tiny islands of Midway, Wake, and Guam, to Manila in the Philippines. Towards the end of 1936, passenger service was introduced on this route, and the next year S-42s carried traffic on an additional leg from the Philippines to Hong Kong. They also went on to start a new route from Hawaii to New Zealand.

French and German Endeavors

In May 1935, the French liner *Normandie* made her maiden voyage across the Atlantic, breaking the speed record. Her crossing time was four days, three hours.

It was the French who were the first to operate airmail services from a ship, employing a catapult on the poop of the liner *Ile de France*. A small single-engined flying boat was launched at sea during the liner's regular Atlantic crossings, starting in 1928. By taking to the air well before the ship's arrival in New York or Le Havre, mail could be delivered in a day less than the time taken by the liner.

The French focused their attention on the narrowest part of the ocean, the 1,900-mile jump from Dakar in Senegal to Natal on the extreme eastern tip of Brazil. They developed a flying boat service carrying mail, not passengers, from Marseilles via Dakar, Natal, and Rio de Janeiro to Buenos Aires. First to go into service, on the last day of 1933, was the graceful prototype Latécoère 300. Roughly the same size as a Martin M-130, though built four years earlier, *Croix du Sud* made twenty-two crossings before being lost at sea. Three later aircraft of the same type carried on with mail delivery to South America until 1940. A second type designed to the same Air Ministry specifications, the Blériot 5190, failed to match the range and load-carrying performance of the Latécoère. One example, named *Santos Dumont* in honor of the celebrated Brazilian aviation pioneer, completed thirty round trips before being withdrawn.

During the 1930s, the French also developed landplanes with a view to transatlantic service, and they simultaneously pursued the construction of larger and more capable flying boats. The Latécoère 521, which made her first flight in 1935, was hampered by inadequate engines. Larger than the Laté 300, the first one crossed the Atlantic to Brazil and visited New York, but it was damaged in Pensacola by a hurricane and neither she nor a sister ship ever entered regular service.

Prototypes of three much larger six-motored flying boat designs were ordered by the French government in 1938, the first of which, the Latécoère 631, did not make her maiden flight until 1942, during the German occupation. This rakish aircraft went into production and three of them finally entered service with Air France in 1947. By this time, American aero engines were available and the performance of the final type was impressive. The largest, most luxurious, and by far the most stylish flying boats ever to enter service, 631s flew the route from Bordeaux via West Africa to Martinique, but only for about a year. The time for flying boats had come and gone: the operation proved to be completely uneconomical.

The German aircraft industry contributed greatly to the evolution of civil aviation. Much German effort was devoted to airships (dirigibles, as distinct from blimps, which are non-rigid craft). From 1933 to 1937, the *Graf Zeppelin* operated a monthly service between Germany and South America, and the larger *Hindenburg* made ten round trips from Frankfurt to New York in the summer of 1936. Her first North Atlantic crossing in 1937, however, ended in fiery disaster at Lakehurst, New Jersey, and this brought the airship program to an end.

An enormous experimental flying boat, the Dornier Do X, caused a sensation by taking to the air in 1929 with 170 passengers. Two years later she made a crossing of the South Atlantic and visited New York, but was hard pressed to complete the journey back to Germany. The design concept, however, which included a battery of no less than twelve engines, proved to be in advance of currently available engine technology.

Following the French, the Germans mounted catapults on two transatlantic liners in 1929. The technique helped to solve the problem of range limitation, for a greater payload could be catapulted aloft than could be achieved by takeoff from the water. In the following year, Dornier Wal flying boats were used in catapult experiments in the South Atlantic. Refueling on board ship in mid-ocean, they were launched into the air and then flew for as long as twelve hours at no more than thirty feet above the sea. These aircraft exploited the so-called "ground effect," deriving additional lift from the cushion of air formed between wings and water.

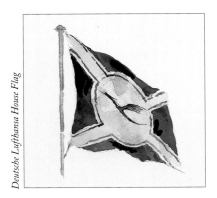

In 1934, Dornier Wals, operating from ships, began an airmail link to Brazil across the narrow part of the South Atlantic. The rest of the route between Berlin and Buenos Aires was flown by a series of landplanes. After 1935, they were joined by another Dornier flying boat type, the extraordinarily graceful little Do 18. The newer airplane was powered by two diesel engines mounted in tandem in a single nacelle.

In the summer months of 1937 and 1938, Do 18 boats operated one sector of an experimental airmail service from Berlin to New York, in combination with landplanes and Blohm & Voss Ha 139 floatplanes. Depot ships equipped with catapults were stationed in the Azores and in Long Island Sound to provide launching platforms for the floatplanes.

Two examples of the Do 26, successor to the Do 18, were employed for a few weeks late in 1938 on the service to South America. This was a larger airplane, comparable in size to the Martin M-130 and the Latécoère 300. The Do 26 had four liquid-cooled six-cylinder diesel engines, a svelte design and high wing-loading. The outcome was an astonishingly long range: 5,500 miles without payload. There was no passenger accommodation. Some three hundred production models of the Do 18, Do 24, and Do 26 were built for military use during the war.

Like the French, the Germans had a bigger six-engined flying boat in the works for the North Atlantic route. This boat, the Blohm & Voss BV 222, never saw commercial service, but fourteen of them went to war in the Luftwaffe in 1941.

Deutsche Lufthansa startled the aviation industry by accomplishing a round-trip flight from Berlin to New York with a Focke-Wulf Fw 200 Condor landplane in August 1938. This was a slim, four-engined airliner capable of carrying twenty-six passengers over 1,000 miles, or nine over a distance of 2,500 miles, and it was far faster than any flying boat. The Condor's engines were American Pratt & Whitney Hornets, built under license in Germany. Its cruising speed was 220 mph at 12,000 feet, and in the coming years it was to prove a deadly menace by shadowing wartime convoys. This flight pointed the way to landplanes as the eventual means of transatlantic service.

The "Empire" Boats

In addition to Pan American, the other main player in the overseas airline business was Imperial Airways. A smaller operation than the American firm, in 1932 it had thirty-two aircraft and earned $250,000, compared to 120 planes and a profit of $700,000. Imperial, however, had a much longer route mileage.

Eight of Imperial's fleet were Handley Page 42s of the *Heracles* class, the world's largest in their day. Eight more were flying boats, of which the latest were three Short Kents called *Scipio*, *Sylvanus*, and *Satyrus*. Both types were four-engined biplanes, capacious in accommodation and leisurely in performance, and both gained a reputation for reliability. In all their years of operation

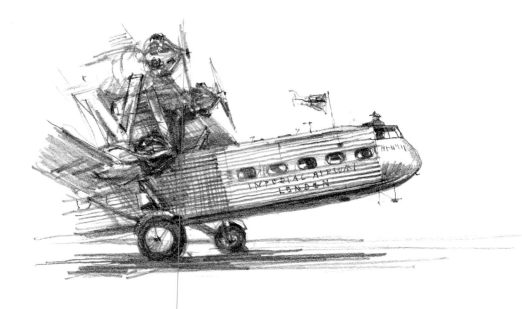

A landplane of the Heracles *class with the Civil Air Ensign raised above the cockpit.*

22

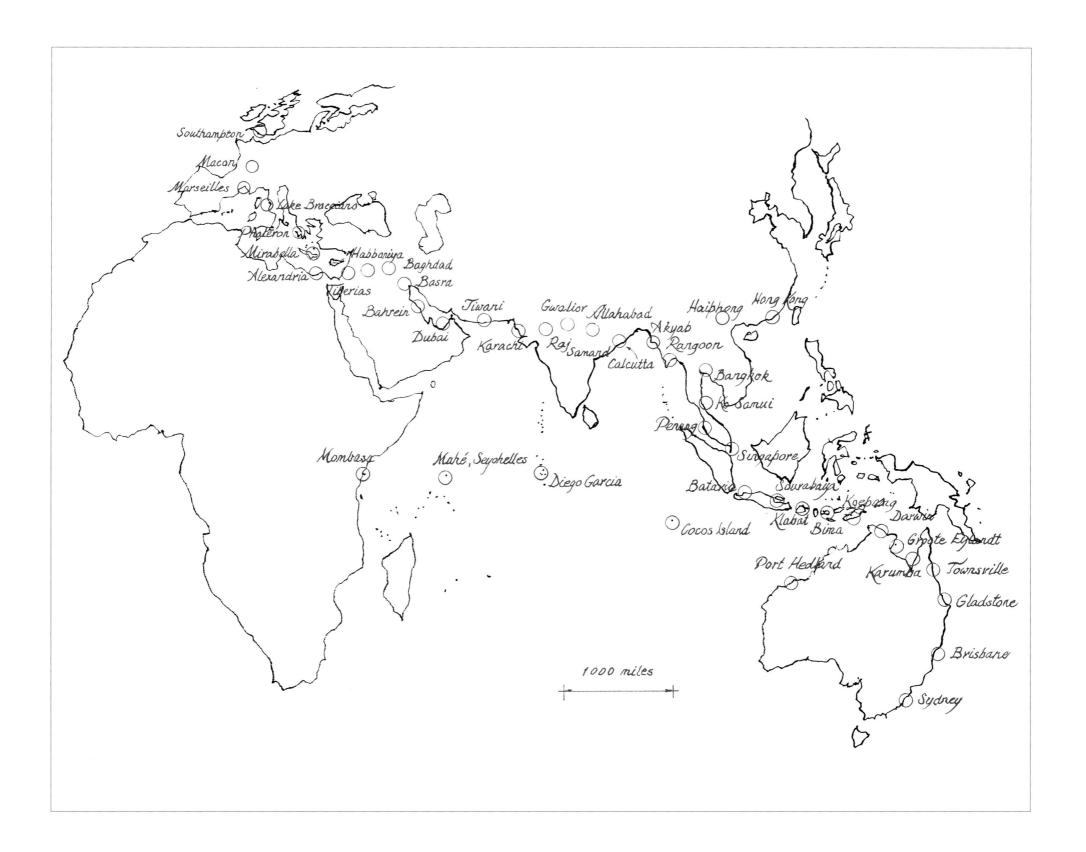

tion, the HP 42s never had a fatal accident and the Kents had but one bad landing, in which two people lost their lives.

The airline's network spread throughout Europe, Africa, the Middle East, India, and the Orient. By 1934, the network extended as far as Australia and Hong Kong. Stages, however, were short. It took more than two weeks to fly from London to Brisbane, with overnight stops, and the average hop between landing fields was only 350 miles. Facing a stiff headwind, it was said, the *Heracles* could be outstripped by a railroad train. Juan Trippe commented with some scorn on the unhurried pace of his flight from Hong Kong to London in 1936.

In 1934, Parliament authorized the Post Office to put into effect the Empire Air Mail Scheme, whereby mail would be carried throughout the empire by air for the same postage rate per half-ounce as domestic mail within the British Isles. At last, it seemed, Imperial Airways could look forward to a major source of revenue, and a predictable one, more in keeping with the scale of the contracts awarded to Pan American by the US Postal Service.

The company promptly ordered twenty-eight Short C-class "Empire" flying boats. Apparently there was little hesitation about choosing flying boats to replace landplanes. The alternative, having to build or enlarge dozens of airports in over thirty countries, was considered unacceptable. Performance had to be good enough for takeoff at high altitudes coupled with high temperatures in Central and East Africa, and takeoff runs in some locations were severely restricted. Nevertheless, few of the destinations were far from some body of water; often it was a busy seaport, but in many places it was a reservoir, lake, or river.

The first of the fleet, called *Canopus*, went into service late in 1936. They were handsome, streamlined aircraft with a cruising speed of 165 mph, and they could carry up to twenty-four passengers in considerable comfort. The passenger accommodation was spacious; it was arranged, as on a yacht, in a series of compartments a few steps up from one another within the tapering lines of the hull. The principal compartment included a "promenade deck," for viewing the world below, and berths were provided for overnight stages. Cabin service was deft and attentive, familiar to those accustomed to First Class passage on mailships of the Union Castle Line or the P&O. Designed to meet the needs of existing services throughout Africa, the Middle East, and the

Orient, the operating range of the Short boats was no more than eight hundred miles.

The "Empire" boats, with their classical names—*Cassiopeia, Coriolanus, Capricornus,* and *Calpurnia*—were splendidly patrician. A total of forty-two were built, including nine for Australian and New Zealand operators. They were intended to brace the central nervous system of the empire. Between Southampton and Sydney they made up to thirty-five scheduled stops (some of them "request stops," as if they were buses), and beyond that they connected to Auckland in New Zealand and eventually to small islands such as Fiji. In the Far East, they flew as far as Hong Kong. The African route included twenty possible boarding stations between Alexandria and Durban. At Auckland the "Empire" C-class boats kissed noses with Pan Am's Clippers out of San Francisco.

For airmail service to Canada, Imperial Airways' intention was to use small long-range floatplanes, which would be carried aloft on the back of a parent flying boat and launched at cruising altitude with a full load of fuel. Designed in 1932, the four-engined *Mercury* eventually carried the mails from Ireland to Montreal in July 1938. By a hairsbreadth, this could be reckoned the first commercial airplane flight across the North Atlantic (after the *Hindenburg*), but this purely mailplane project was then abandoned. The aircraft achieved some remarkable flights, including one of 6,000 miles nonstop from Scotland to South Africa.

Serious attention was also devoted to the idea of flight refueling. In 1932, Sir Alan Cobham founded a company to develop the technique, and by 1939 the airline was able to start operating a regular mail service directly from Southampton to Montreal. Four "Empire" boats were employed, being refueled in the air over Shannon in Western Ireland and over Botwood, Newfoundland, on the return. It was intended to start passenger service on June 1, 1939, but the airline decided that the technique was too uncertain yet for passenger traffic, and on account of the war the service was discontinued in October 1940.

Experiments were revived after the war, and in 1951 flight refueling was tried again in order to prolong the range of the thirsty early jets. It has since been developed with important military applications, and is currently used to project air power worldwide.

Transatlantic landplanes were also considered, and Imperial placed an order for an airliner called the Albatross. Built by de Havilland using wooden stressed skin construction, this beautiful little airplane failed to meet long-distance performance expectations, but six of them went into service on European routes in 1938. Once again, it was mainly the engines that were lacking; the technology of glued wooden construction was vindicated in the strikingly successful Mosquito high-speed bomber, built by de Havilland during the war.

In 1935, the British Air Ministry finally acknowledged that it had neglected to address the critical need for a boat with transatlantic range. Expenditure was authorized on a very much larger, more powerful version of the "Empire" boat, the G-class, three of which were slated for completion in 1939. The G-class boats were very close to going into passenger service when the war came, but we now know that the airline considered that their payload on the North Atlantic would have been only marginally profitable. Imperial Airways would probably have felt obliged to go ahead anyway.

As it happened, development delays (engines again) meant that the first of the type, *Golden Hind*, was not delivered until October, a month after the outbreak of the Second World War. She and her sister ships were drafted into military service, although *Golden Hind* was returned within a year and operated between Poole, Foynes, and Lisbon for much of the war.

With the outbreak of war, the government stopped work on all civilian aircraft projects, and the entire aircraft industry was turned to the production of combat aircraft in a fight for national survival.

It is well to emphasize that in 1939 the prospect of transatlantic flying held anxieties that are now forgotten. There was a real possibility of engine failure in mid-ocean, and the chances of alighting safely on water in a landplane, and being rescued, were not promising. During the darkest time of the war, in the winter of 1940, seemingly desperate risks were taken to fly Lockheed Hudsons from Gander, in Newfoundland, to Aldergrove in Northern Ireland. (The Hudson was a military version of of the Lockheed 14 Super Electra, a twin-engine airliner. It was ordered by the RAF in 1939 for maritime patrol duties, British factories being fully engaged in building other types of combat aircraft.) Gradually, these transatlantic flights became routine. More and more crossings were made to deliver warplanes, and a ferry service was inaugurated to return the pilots, many of them women. The aircraft employed on the return leg were RAF Consolidated B-24 Liberator bombers, specially modified for ocean flying. They were described as VLR, for very long range, and the same type was used to good effect in anti-submarine operations. By 1945, thousands of people had flown across the Atlantic, and perceptions had completely changed.

Transatlantic Passenger Service

To return to the theme, the first real transatlantic aircraft was the Boeing 314. Pan American's success in bringing about the design and production of this big flying boat, and the airline's expertise in operating it safely and profitably over ocean trade routes, led all others in the evolution of long distance civil aviation. The performance specifications of the 314 were spelled out largely by Trippe himself, always thinking in advance of what was currently achievable, and the design team was spurred on by what was once described as the "shameless tenacity" of André Priester. Realizing that the M-130 lacked

Passenger cabin in an "Empire" boat, with dark green leather seats and beige linen curtains. Carpet and ceiling were pale green.

the stride to master the Atlantic, Pan American had sent out invitations to aircraft builders as soon as the three Martin boats had been delivered in 1935. Glenn Martin and Igor Sikorsky considered that they were due an opportunity to develop existing designs under contract, but Trippe disagreed. An engineer at the Boeing company in Seattle had an idea to exploit the newly available 1,000 hp Wright Cyclone engine and the splendid new wing which Boeing had developed for the B-15 bomber (later to evolve into the B-17). Starting with these, the Boeing management took a chance, and rashly offered to build six flying boats of entirely new design within a period of seventeen months. Boeing was stepping out into a new field, and it underestimated the task. In the long run, however, the risk paid off. It was this project that put the firm in line to become, twenty years later, the world's premier supplier of large passenger aircraft.

Several major difficulties were encountered in development of the Boeing 314. Not until early in 1939 did the first of the six become available for airline service. Meanwhile, six more had been ordered. The small numbers need to be emphasized. Only twelve of the type were built, and in all the world there were only a few dozen long-range aircraft at that time.

The first of the Boeings, *Yankee Clipper*, started scheduled transatlantic operation on May 20, 1939, and passenger service was inaugurated in June. The starting point was Port Washington, on Long Island Sound, about fourteen miles east of New York. One year later, flying was moved to the new La Guardia Airport, some ten miles closer to the city. Soon after takeoff on the first passenger flight, a steward passed through the airplane handing out passenger lists, and the twenty-two passengers were free to move around and make themselves acquainted. Dinner was laid out on linen tablecloths in one compartment, and while it was being served, stewards made up the sleeping berths elsewhere. The flight went via the Azores (where it was noted that dirty crockery couldn't be taken ashore for dishwashing because of objections by Portuguese customs officials). Only a half-dozen trips were accomplished to Marseilles, and the same number to Southampton, before the skies over France and Britain became a war zone.

Virgin Islands Seaplane Shuttle

Marine Air Terminal built by Imperial Airways on Southampton Docks, destroyed during World War II

The War Years

Pan American's Boeing Clippers maintained a transatlantic service during the war years, starting sometimes from Long Island Sound (La Guardia), and sometimes from Baltimore to be free of danger from ice. In the severe winter of 1940, even Baltimore froze over, and flights had to originate in Miami for a time. Because of ice, poor visibility, and stormy winter weather, they used the direct route by way of Newfoundland to Ireland only in summer. The Clippers mostly flew via Bermuda, or sometimes direct to the Azores, and thence to Lisbon, which became a wartime rendezvous for refugees, diplomats, journalists, and spies. The Republic of Ireland, like Portugal, managed to remain neutral, so for much of the war the big boats continued northwards across the Bay of Biscay to Foynes, on the River Shannon in the west of Ireland. Quietly and unobtrusively, they would go about their business after dark, conveying vital dispatches and VIPs to this insignificant village amidst the green pastoral landscape of County Limerick.

Foynes is situated on the banks of the meandering River Shannon, surrounded by shallow waterways. Once in a while, a pilot would alight on the water only to find himself bounded by unfamiliar fields. The routine was to wait for daylight, and then motor around looking for a local farmhand, who would be hailed from the cockpit to give shouted directions.

Boeing 314s flew on many extraordinary missions. They carried artillery proximity fuses to Liberia destined for the British Army in the Middle East; they flew secretly to Léopoldville to bring back uranium for making atomic bombs; they explored island bases in the western part of the Indian Ocean; and they carried aircraft tires to Calcutta for the P-40s of Chennault's Flying Tigers. When the Japanese bombed Pearl Harbor, one of the big boats was caught en route to New Zealand, and she made an epic journey back westwards around the world. High octane spirit was scarcer than hen's teeth, and *Pacific Clipper* made the journey home partly on regular auto gasoline, coupled with the determination and disciplined skill of the aircrew.

These few airplanes were a critical link in the worldwide chain of resources which were steadily being mobilized into action against the Axis pow-

ers. While visiting London in June 1941 to deliver a lecture at the Royal Aeronautical Society, Juan Trippe was summoned to visit the prime minister. The main subject of his talk with Winston Churchill was the possibility of setting up an air supply route via West Africa to Cairo, where British forces in the Western Desert were hard pressed against Italian and German armies. Part of the conversation touched on the Boeing 314. He was summoned to the White House on his return, where the president approved the sale of three of Pan American's precious 314s to Britain. It is chilling to realize that, in the event of Portugal being subjected to German occupation, the Boeings were the only airplanes capable of maintaining an oceanic link between Britain and the free world. With General Franco's fascist regime firmly in charge of Spain, this seemed at the time a likely scenario.

Churchill himself took the controls of *Berwick,* one of these British 314s, during his return flight from America via Bermuda in January 1942, and US President Franklin D. Roosevelt used a Boeing 314 to fly to the Casablanca Conference twelve months later. This was the first time a president had ever flown abroad while in office.

A planeload of impatient passengers was occasionally stranded for more than two weeks in Bermuda, waiting for the ocean swell to subside at their next stop, the Azores. The station manager was at his wits' end devising golf tournaments and bridge contests to divert the generals, congressmen, cardinals, and treasury officials who became irritable at being detained.

Many of Imperial Airways' "Empire" boats were called up for military service, but those that remained in civilian use operated the "Horseshoe Route" from Durban, South Africa, through the Middle East, India, and the East Indies to Australia. The direct linkage via Cairo and across Europe was severed early in the war, and with the fall of France, all flights had to be re-routed via Lisbon. So the British, too, quietly operated their wartime courier service out of Foynes, in the soft drizzle of western Ireland, through Lisbon to Bathurst in the West African colony of Gambia, and thence via the Gold Coast, Nigeria, the Congo, and Equatorial Africa to Khartoum, where it connected with the Horseshoe. The wartime link from Britain to Foynes was maintained by RAF flying boats out of Poole, in the south of England.

The top brass wore civilian clothes on these flights, and no munitions were carried. In Lisbon, pilots would find themselves mingling with Lufthansa crews freshly arrived from Berlin. Portugal had been allied to Britain since a treaty of mutual assistance signed in 1293; it suited both belligerents to ignore the other and not to upset the delicate status quo.

Coda

The rest of the flying boat story is marked *diminuendo.*

During the war, two great types of flying boats performed Trojan service for the Allies. One was the Consolidated PBY, named Catalina by the British, which won affection as much for its quirky good looks as for its extraordinarily robust construction. It was essentially a military airplane, although a few have been put to civilian use. A PBY marked with the seahorse emblem of Air France was photographed over Rio de Janeiro in 1998.

The second was the Short Sunderland, a warplane derived from the design of the "Empire" boats. She was not a sleek looking aircraft, but proved to be one of the most effective weapons systems in dealing with U-boats. After the war, twenty-eight Sunderlands were converted to civilian use, and an improved civilian version called the Solent went into production. These joined

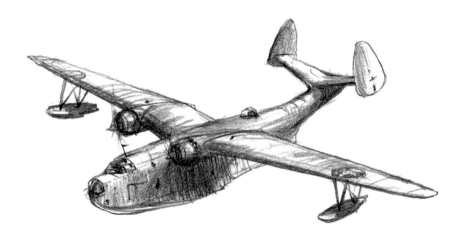

Martin PBM-3 Mariner. 118 ft wingspan, range 2,400 miles. About 1,370 were built in the years 1940-49, the second most numerous flying boat produced. Used as a patrol bomber, transport, and for anti-submarine warfare.

Howard Hughes to build a truly monstrous cargo plane that would evade all submarines. Kaiser, of course, was the creator of the mighty Liberty ship building program, but wartime priorities determined the use of laminated birch for construction of the aircraft. The shipping emergency was over roughly four years before the first flying boat was ready, but Hughes alone determined to complete the prototype H-4 and to make it fly. That he succeeded, with himself at the controls for a flight of just about a mile, is a matter of legend.

The Japanese surrender took place on September 2, 1945, and before the end of the year Pan American ceased its flying boat operations. Wartime development of the C-54 military transport culminated in the production of well over a thousand. The company had placed orders as early as 1940, and by the end of 1945, the USAAF had released ten. Known in civilian life as the Douglas DC-4, no less than ninety-two were delivered to the airline before the end of 1950, closely followed by the pressurized Lockheed Constellation, deliveries of which began early in 1946. Landplanes displaced flying boats on oceanic routes.

So the Marine Air Terminal at Dinner Key was sold, and it became (and remains to this day) Miami City Hall. The wonderful Boeing 314 had its swan song when the last surviving example, having been sold to an inexperienced charter operator, ran out of fuel and ditched ignominiously in the mid-Atlantic. Fortunately, the flying boat was able to alight near a weather ship, and all on board were safely rescued in spite of heavy seas.

Of course, this is not all. Passenger flying boat services, albeit mostly with smaller boats such as the Grumman Goose and Mallard, continued for some time in Alaska, the southwest Pacific, to Madeira, the Bahamas, and in the Caribbean until Hurricane Hugo demolished the last of that fleet in 1989. During the Cold War, Short Sunderlands were pressed into use as colliers, delivering coal to Havel See as part of the Berlin Airlift. Several enormous Martin Mars boats continued to operate in British Columbia on fire fighting service as late as the 1990s, and small flying boats can still be found operating out of Miami to Key West, the very first place from which Pan American Airways flew in 1927.

some of the old "Empire" boats which were still flying for Imperial's successor, British Overseas Airways Corporation (BOAC). Eighteen Solents were built, some of which continued to be used on BOAC's African routes up until 1950, and the type was still in service in New Zealand and Australia as late as 1974. A Sunderland conversion with a remarkable *curriculum vitae* can be seen in the air museum at Southampton.

Two other types of flying boats were widely used by the allies. By far the most numerous, next to the PBY, was the Martin PBM-3 Mariner, which performed with distinction in both main theaters of war as a patrol bomber and as a transport. The Consolidated PB2Y-2 Coronado also saw extensive war service, mainly as a transport.

Sikorsky, now amalgamated with Vought, built a truly transoceanic flying boat, the VS-44, three of which went into service with American Export Airlines in 1942. They were just capable of flying from Foynes to New York direct. One of them has been most beautifully restored and is on show at the New England Air Museum near Hartford, Connecticut.

The Hughes H-4 *Spruce Goose* deserves mention because, I have discovered, for many people she is the only flying boat they have heard about. During the worst of the U-boat campaign, when ships carrying supplies across the Atlantic were being sunk in dreadful numbers, Henry J. Kaiser engaged with

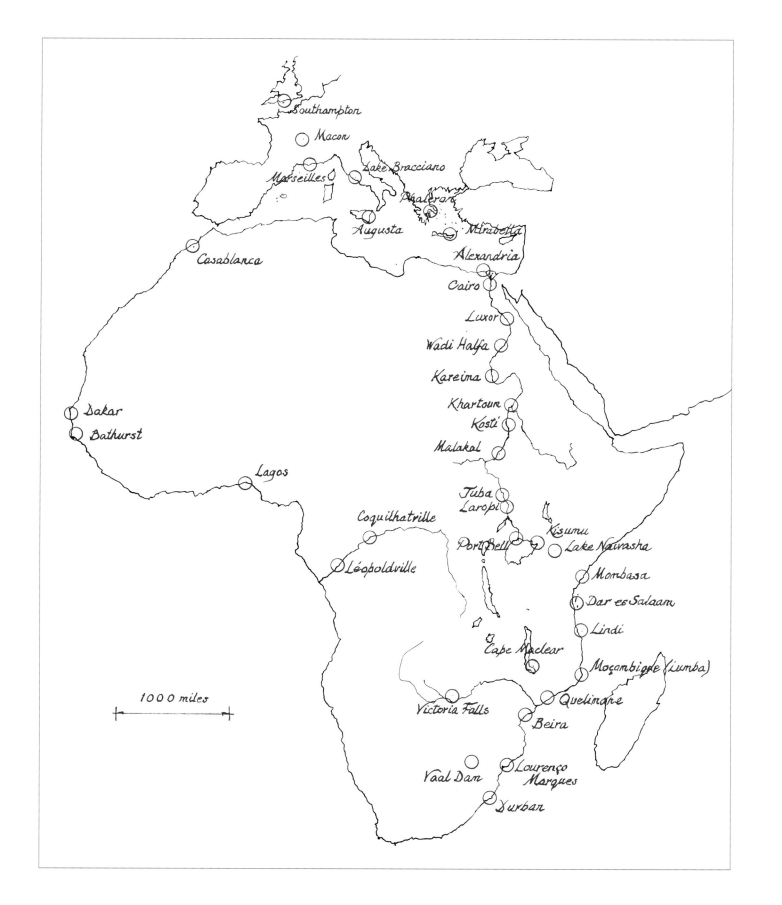

PLATE 1.

NC-4 at Horta, in the Azores Islands,
during the first Atlantic crossing by air, 1919

There is no classier department store than John Wanamaker's in Philadelphia. In 1914, Rodman Wanamaker, heir to the fortune, commissioned the aviation pioneer Glenn Curtiss to design and build a flying boat to cross the Atlantic. Curtiss is credited with the idea of incorporating a "step" in the hull to aid in achieving takeoff, and he benefited from the work of a celebrated yacht designer, W. Starling Burgess, who devised suitable hull forms and built marine aircraft at his boatyard in Marblehead, Massachusetts. The outcome was an airplane called the *America*, which Curtiss built at Hammondsport, on Lake Keuka, one of the finger lakes in New York State. *America* was an impressive project, although it failed to achieve its objective in that year.

John Porte, a retired British naval officer, was closely associated with the design. With the outbreak of war in Europe, he returned to England, where he took part in the evolution of the Short F-5 Felixstowe, a successful wartime flying boat which in turn became the basis for development of the Curtiss F-5L of 1918.

Curtiss, meanwhile, developed a series of boats derived from work on the *America*, culminating in the H-12 and the H-16, which were used by the US Navy. The Navy established its own aircraft factory at the Philadelphia Navy Yard to manufacture both the H-16 and the F-5L. In 1918 it entered into a joint contract with Curtiss to develop a boat capable of flying across the Atlantic. The type was named NC (Navy Curtiss), hence "Nancy," and four boats were constructed in the series, NC-1 to NC-4.

The four airplanes were commissioned into the US Navy as Seaplane Division One. Three of them made their way from New York to Halifax and thence to Newfoundland. Together they took off from Trepassey Bay on May 16, 1919 and headed southeast across 1,500 miles of ocean towards Horta in the Azores Islands. This route was chosen because it encompassed the shortest individual segments on the transatlantic crossing. The Navy stationed warships at fifty-mile intervals along the way to help with navigation. NC-1 lost her way and had to alight on open water to be able to use radio direction-finding equipment. She was unable to get airborne again and was eventually abandoned. NC-3 suffered a similar fate, but managed to taxi to the Azores under her own power. NC-4 made it all the way, achieving the harbor at Horta in fifteen hours' flying time from Newfoundland. After a break of ten days, she and her crew of six flew without further incident to Ponta Delgada, thence to Lisbon, Figueira, Ferrol, and finally to Plymouth, in southwest England. NC-4, the first airplane to cross the Atlantic Ocean, now rests at the Naval Air Museum in Pensacola, Florida, on loan from the Smithsonian Institution.

Compared to other aircraft of her day, NC-4 owed much of her success to the power, economy, and reliability of her four Liberty engines. Two were mounted back-to-back on the centerline, a tractor and a pusher, and two more tractors flanked the central nacelle. They were twelve-cylinder v-motors, water cooled, each producing 400 horsepower. The type was designed in response to government initiative immediately after the United States entered the war in 1917. Twenty thousand Liberty engines were made before 1926, and they powered the great majority of American aircraft of that era.

PLATE 2.

Curtiss F-5L at the Casa Marina Hotel, Key West, 1922

In November 1919, Aeromarine Airways Inc. began flying passengers from Key West—operating from a waterfront lot between Duval and Simonton Streets—to Havana. Surplus World War I Curtiss F-5L flying boats were employed, and ex-Navy pilots were engaged to fly the machines. The planes were remodeled by the company into fourteen-seater Model 75 Aeromarine Cruisers, with two cabins, one for non-smokers. The pilot sat up high in the open air amidships.

Back in 1912, Henry Flagler had completed the extension of the Florida East Coast Railroad for one hundred miles beyond Miami, bridging from one Key to another until it reached Key West. His ambition was to make this the jumping-off point for steamer connections to all the islands of the Caribbean, and to Panama. He built a fine hotel, the Casa Marina, close to the southernmost tip of the island. Aeromarine's flying boat *Columbus* is portrayed here in the shallow waters off the hotel, paying a visit no doubt for publicity purposes. The Key West Athletic Club is in the background.

Under owner Inglis Uppercu's direction, Aeromarine manufactured aero engines and aircraft of its own and other companies' designs. Its airline operations extended from New York to Detroit, Cleveland, Miami, and Nassau before it had to close at the end of 1923. Offshore destinations were particularly popular during the period of Prohibition, and a few flights originating in New York were dubbed the "Highball Express."

The Key West railroad was destroyed in the great hurricane that struck the Keys on September 2, 1935. It was never rebuilt, and many of the bridges and causeways that linked the islands were used to create a road connection between the mainland and Key West. Disused sections of the works can still be seen along the way.

PLATE 3.

Short Singapore 1 of Sir Alan Cobham
at Port Bell, Uganda, 1927

Twenty Thousand Miles in a Flying Boat, Sir Alan Cobham's account of his survey flight throughout the length of Africa, is a real period piece. In courteous and humorous terms he describes a world of unspoiled wilderness, animated by massive herds of game. Along the way he encounters generous and cheerful people, in what by all accounts is a well-ordered world. Conditions were certainly primitive, but it is a far cry from the calamitous picture we receive today of many of the countries on his journey.

Cobham's craft is pictured on Lake Victoria, at the tiny port which serves Kampala, capital of Uganda. The airplane was imperiled by eager Buganda warriors in dugout canoes who congregated around it in welcome as it came to rest. A heavy mokoro dugout could easily have punctured the Singapore's hull.

Like other pilots who followed, Sir Alan had his share of adventures with the wildlife which populated the waters on which he tried to land. He and his wife also suffered grievously from insects and terrific heat in the southern Sudan, and his aircraft from barnacles which clung to the bottom when it was stranded for a time in salt water in West Africa. Predictably, most of their difficulties arose from mechanical failures and in trying to arrange for fuel in remote locations, but they were received everywhere with dignified hospitality.

Pusher and tractor engines back-to-back on a Savoia-Marchetti S.55

PLATE 4.

Short S 8 Calcutta alighting at Corfu, 1929

Gerald Durrell, in *My Family and Other Animals,* gives a wonderful description of a flying boat landing. On Thursday afternoons, the weekly Imperial Airways Short Calcutta would land at Corfu, en route from Brindisi to Athens. Corfu was used by Imperial Airways as a staging post during the years 1929–1932, and occasionally thereafter. Gerald and his friend Dr. Theodore Stephanides would eagerly watch its arrival in the bay below the Durrell house.

The only part of the house from which one could see the actual touchdown was the attic. Invariably, it seems, aircraft engines would be heard in the middle of afternoon tea, whereupon the whole family would unceremoniously leave the table and race upstairs. Leaning out of a dormer window, the children gazed down onto a placid stretch of sea, framed by the tops of olive trees. The flying boat slowly dropped lower and lower. "Suddenly it would be over the water, racing its reflection over the blue surface." Seconds later, it lightly touched the surface with a splash of white foam, and then finally settled into the water, leaving furrows behind as it gradually slowed down in its course across the bay.

Theodore's appraisal was always the same. "Um . . . yes," he would say, "it certainly is a very . . . er . . . *enjoyable* sight."

The Short brothers, Oswald and Eustace, were licensed in 1909 to build Wright flying machines. During World War I, the company built the most widely-used Allied naval aircraft types, and after the demise in the 1930s of the French Blériot and Farman companies, the Short brothers advertised themselves, with some justice, as the world's oldest aircraft manufacturer.

The Imperial Airways Short Calcutta had something of the grace of a wildfowl

PLATE 5.

Consolidated Commodore of NYRBA over Rio de Janeiro, 1930

The New York, Rio and Buenos Aires Line was founded in 1929 to operate down the east coasts of North and South America, with a branch line across the Andes to Santiago, Chile. Passengers would travel from New York to Miami by train, and from there to Buenos Aires by air with thirty-two ports-of-call en route. The full journey took ten days.

The company purchased several Sikorsky S-38s and Ford Tri-Motors, but the principal aircraft to be used on the coastal route was the Consolidated Commodore. This design was based on that of a Navy patrol plane, the XP2Y-1. The civilian version had twenty-two seats, twin 575 hp Pratt & Whitney Hornet engines, a speed of 108 mph and an operating range of up to about 600 miles. NYRBA ordered fourteen of them.

Casting off the mooring on a Consolidated Commodore called for dexterity

President of the airline was Ralph O'Neill, a brilliant World War I pilot, who later became a salesman for Boeing. He was loud, energetic, and effective, but he was not a careful man. O'Neill piloted the survey flights himself, and the first months of operation early in 1930 were distinctly erratic. Much hinged on the award of air mail contracts, and while O'Neill barnstormed through South America to sign up, he unwisely negotiated unacceptably low rates for mail contracts with South American countries, and neglected to pay enough attention to US Postal Service requirements. The system was that foreign payments to airlines had to be passed on to the postal service to offset the subsidy that was given to US carriers. Pan Am's president, Juan Trippe, outmaneuvered O'Neill in Washington, and when the stock market collapsed the principal shareholders in NYRBA sold out to Pan Am.

In the painting, the famous Copacabana Beach on the Atlantic coast can be seen directly underneath the Commodore. In the 1920s, the Copacabana Palace Hotel was the ritziest place in Brazil. In one moment of exuberance, O'Neill evidently made a power dive aimed directly at the hotel, to the astonishment of its fashionable clientele who were dallying with daiquiris on the terrace.

The plane's remarkable color scheme was concocted by O'Neill himself. The fuselage was cream, and wings, tailplane, the bottom part of the hull and the trim around the windows were painted what he called "coral." Recent research indicates that this was actually an orange color rather than pink.

One detail about the airplane is worth mention. Beneath the wings is a pair of small, conical objects outboard of the engines. These are electrical generators. It was mechanically simpler to generate power by tiny wind-driven propellers than to couple the generators directly to the main engines.

PLATE 6.

Short S 17 Kent Scipio *coming in to alight at Alexandria, 1931*

Imperial Airways used three Kent-class flying boats between 1931 and 1935 to operate across the Mediterranean. They flew between Brindisi and Alexandria, stopping at Corfu, at Phaleron, near Athens, and at Mirabella on the island of Crete. They carried fifteen passengers in a rather spacious and comfortably furnished cabin. The airplanes were powered by four Bristol Jupiter engines, which permitted a cruising speed of 100 mph.

At Alexandria, the flying boats alighted in the busy harbor in front of the Summer Palace at Ras-el-Tin. Often they would find themselves surrounded by Royal Navy warships of the Mediterranean Fleet. *Scipio* is seen here circling before touchdown. Egyptian buildings have a disappointing grayish hue, not the clean, golden sand color that one tends to imagine in the desert.

Once they reached Egypt, all passengers—whether bound for the Middle East, India, and beyond, or headed southwards towards East Africa—had to transfer to landplanes. The European sector of the journey was complicated by Mussolini's refusal to allow flights over Italy, so passengers had to fly from London to Basel and travel from there to Brindisi by train. This difficulty was finally overcome in June 1934.

Comfortable-looking cabin in a Short Kent

PLATE 7.

Sikorsky S-40 Caribbean Clipper *at Panama City, 1931*

Pan American Airways had the Sikorsky S-40 designed and built to suit its own operational requirements, a first in the US aviation industry. Juan Trippe, founder and president of the airline, was proud of his family background in shipping. It was his initiative to name this and all subsequent PAA airliners Clippers, and to adopt naval uniforms and terminology. Three of the type were built, the first one christened *American Clipper* by Mrs. Herbert Hoover when it was delivered to the airline in 1931.

The S-40 was a much enlarged edition of the successful S-38, and like the smaller plane, it was designed and operated at first as an amphibian. This gave it the capacity to work from airfields as well as from the water, but as time went on the weight of landing gear was recognized as a penalty and wheels were abandoned. It was a four-engined monoplane with a roomy fuselage capable of seating thirty-eight passengers in what was called "a real sexy interior," paneled in fumed oak.

Pierce Arrow sedanca de ville

In its day, the S-40 far surpassed landplanes in load-carrying performance. Its seating capacity was roughly three times that of the contemporary Ford Tri-Motor. The aircraft was intended for operations around and across the Caribbean, the first flight being from Miami to Panama via Cuba, Jamaica, and Colombia. While considered large and flashy in her day, the S-40 was not an object of beauty. One pilot described the type as "a miscellaneous collection of spare parts flying in formation."

PLATE 8.

Latécoère 300 Croix du Sud *alighting at Natal, Brazil, 1934*

The extraordinarily graceful, swanlike form of the Laté 300 *Croix du Sud* has just appeared in the night sky over the southern hemisphere, about to touch the water at the end of a flight from Dakar in Senegal, West Africa. The big four-engined mailplane was remarkable in her day for the ability to lift a weight equal to her own airframe by way of fuel and payload. But the Laté carried no passengers, only mail.

Mail contracts played an essential part in the development of air transportation. In the second quarter of the nineteenth century, steamship companies were formed in Britain to take over from the Post Office the carriage of mail overseas. (Mailships were at first known as packet boats, from the French *paquetbot,* or government dispatch vessel.) Until some time after 1860, steamships were so expensive to operate that passenger or freight revenue alone could not support scheduled services on ocean routes. Mail contracts nurtured the growth of steamship lines.

The United States of America, with its great land mass, was fertile ground for the evolution of airmail. In 1922, the US Postal Service started the construction of light beacons every ten miles across the country, and of emergency airstrips every thirty. In 1927, it introduced a radio navigation system which by 1936 had been adopted nationwide. In the 1920s, the postal service let contracts to individual pilots, and by 1926 it had started placing mail contracts for trunk routes with air transport companies.

Domestic mail by air was never a factor in European countries, but international airmail was another matter. Political and economic considerations lay behind each country's policy on airmail, and on the concession of landing and traffic rights. Mail contracts were recognized as a key to the growth of national air services, and to the expansion of trade. Ambitious nations regarded the promotion of their own overseas air mail carriers as a matter of public policy.

In the US, an enlightened and enterprising postal service did much to foster the preeminence of American civil aviation, and the placing of substantial contracts with Pan American Airways supported the growth of overseas operations. In Europe, each country likewise favored a national carrier—in some cases with government participation—and subsidies were devoted to the development of domestic aircraft types and to the creation of international air routes. Before the Second World War, the carriage of passengers overseas was scarcely economic.

PLATE 9.

Consolidated Commodore shortly before alighting at Nassau, Bahama Islands, 1934

Pan American Airways inherited a fleet of fourteen Commodore flying boats when the airline took over NYRBA in 1930. The airplanes had accommodation for up to twenty-two passengers, an operating range of roughly 600 miles, and a cruising speed of 108 mph. With ten passengers, they were capable of flying 1,000 miles. Power was supplied by two Pratt & Whitney engines of 570 hp.

Part of the atmosphere of air travel derived from the hotels along the way. The passengers heading into Nassau may well have spent their last night at the palatial Biltmore Hotel in Coral Gables, Miami. The Miami Biltmore opened its doors in 1926, at the very summit of a giddy boom in Florida real estate. The hotel's owner was George Merrick, developer, promoter, and impresario of the new town of Coral Gables. His fancy in architecture seems to have run along similar lines to that of William Randolph Hearst, and Merrick imported a small fleet of Venetian gondolas to ferry guests to and from Biscayne Bay for the hotel's grand opening.

In the following year, 1927, Pan American Airways was incorporated in Miami. In the decade thereafter, many passengers from the north would arrive by train and stay a few days at the Biltmore before continuing their journey to destinations in the Caribbean, South or Central America.

A very different hotel, which also figures in the flying boat story, is the South-Western Hotel in Southampton, England. Built when the railway reached Southampton in 1840, it has a cameo of the young Queen Victoria on the pediment. Ninety years later, Imperial Airways passengers would travel to the South-Western by special train of Pullman cars, and stay overnight at the hotel before dawn departure by flying boat.

Both buildings can still be seen, fifty years after the flying boats have gone.

Biltmore Hotel, Coral Gables, Miami

The South-Western Hotel, Southampton, still stands, but is no longer used as a hotel

PLATE 10.

Sikorsky S-42, S-38, and S-40 flying boats at Dinner Key, Miami, 1935

This painting depicts three generations of Sikorskys which served Pan American Airways. The first S-38 was built in 1928, and the newly-incorporated airline purchased the second example to emerge from the factory. The type became the mainstay of Pan American's Caribbean network. A grand total of thirty-eight were bought between 1928 and 1934, of which thirteen were delivered to subsidiary companies.

The S-38, shown here in the water, was an amphibian, which is to say it had retractable wheels, enabling it to land on a runway or on water. After a water landing, it could taxi towards a slip and climb ashore. The airplane had eight passenger seats, the engines were two Pratt & Whitney Wasps of 450 hp, and the operating range was just under 600 miles.

The S-40, which can just be discerned in front of the hangar on the right hand side of the painting, was a much enlarged version of the S-38. Only three of them were built, they had four engines, thirty-eight seats, and a range of 900 miles.

The S-42 flying overhead was of an entirely new generation of aircraft. She was designed in response to the operational experience of the Pan Am team in flying her predecessors. The S-42 introduced wing flaps, enabling her

Pan Am ground transportation at Miami was described as the Aero-car and operated by the Red Top Cab Co.

to fly with a much higher wing loading, and her instrumentation was more extensive. She had four Pratt & Whitney Hornet radial motors of 700 hp, and her cruising speed was 150 mph. Seating was for thirty-two passengers, and her normal operating range was 1,200 miles.

In the background is the terminal building built by Pan American at Dinner Key, Miami, which currently serves as Miami City Hall. The hangars are now used by a boat marina.

PLATE 11.

Bréguet 530 Saigon **Algérie** *over the coast of North Africa, 1935*

The French aircraft manufacturer Bréguet built modified versions of the British-designed flying boat called the Short Kent: fifteen military aircraft which were given the name Bizerte; and two of a civilian type named Saigon, which were supplied to Air France. A longer-range derivative, to be called the Dakar, was projected for transatlantic mailplane service, but it never materialized.

The Saigon was unusual in having three classes of passenger accommodation in separate cabins, up to a total of nineteen. *Algérie* and her sister ship *Tunisie* operated routes between Marseilles, Ajaccio, and Tunis, and between Marseilles and Algiers, from May 1934 until 1942. They were equipped with three Hispano-Suiza engines of 785 hp, which gave them a top speed of 150 mph, and their operating range was about 600 miles.

This flying boat is characteristic of many biplane flying boat types built in the 1930s, such as the Short Singapore, Supermarine Stranraer, Blackburn Iris, Martin PM-1, Douglas PD-1, and Consolidated P2Y-3. Note the large wingspan in relation to fuselage length, the broad flared hull, and the complex braced structure linking the wings to fuselage, engines, and floats. Clearly evident is the unequal span of upper and lower wings. In a number of flying boat designs the lower wings were less than half the span of the upper. Some of the Dornier, Martin, and Boeing boats incorporated brief stub wings, or sponsons, situated at water level, to provide stability while the craft was in the water. The term sesquiplane is correctly applied to an airplane with one-and-a-half pairs of wings.

Dornier Wal used on the South Atlantic. Note the enormous loop antenna used for radio direction finding.

PLATE 12.

Sikorsky S-38 **Carnauba** *over the Amazon forest in Brazil, 1935*

The Sikorsky S-38 was Pan American Airways' bread-and-butter airplane. The airline purchased thirty-eight of them, and the type became the workhorse of the company, laying the foundations of its network in the Caribbean and in Central America. It was also used extensively in South America by Pan American and its associated companies, Panagra and Panair do Brasil.

The hull was a wooden-framed slipper, covered in aluminum. The wings and tail were a completely separate upper structure, and were fabric-covered. Most S-38s were amphibians—that is, they could be used on land or on water.

The prototype was built for NYRBA, and went into service in 1928. Pan American ordered the second. Many others were delivered to private owners, such as one that was bought by Martin and Osa Johnson, who used it for pioneering flights in East Africa. Another S-38 was painted in the house colors of the S.C. Johnson Wax Company of Racine, Wisconsin. In 1935, this airplane, called *Carnauba*, was used by Herbert F. Johnson on a 15,000-mile expedition from Milwaukee to Fortaleza in Brazil, to study an area rich in carnauba trees. The carnauba nut was a key ingredient in Johnson Wax. In 1998, the expedition was reenacted by his son, using a replica of the original Sikorsky S-38.

Sikorsky S-38 amphibian

PLATE 13.

Martin M-130 China Clipper *at Wake Island, 1935*

In November 1935, Pan American Airways opened the first Pacific airmail service, using three new Martin M-130 flying boats. They operated out of Alameda in San Francisco Bay, to Honolulu in the Hawaiian Islands. From there they flew on to refuel successively at Midway, Wake, and Guam islands, and finally to Manila Bay in the Philippines. Flights left weekly, and overnight stops were made at each island, resulting in a total journey of five days. The first segment, from San Francisco to Honolulu, was the longest at 2,400 miles, and this is still the longest non-alternative segment on the world's commercial air routes. The Martin covered this distance in an average of eighteen hours, but payload was strictly limited. The mail contract called for 800 pounds, but there was usually no more than about 500 pounds to go. When passenger service was inaugurated eleven months later, the Martins were unable to carry more than eight people on this sector.

Captain Edwin C. Musick, chief pilot of Pan American, was in command of *China Clipper* on the first scheduled flight. On arrival at Manila he was met by a great fleet of boats and cheering crowds. The crew was feted when they reached the shore; they were greeted by a floral arch, a parade in open cars, and a civic banquet. Musick brought a letter from President Franklin D. Roosevelt to President Manuel Quezon and delivered it with a formal speech.

Pan American captains, by and large, were not given to making speeches. In October 1936, Juan Trippe invited a party of celebrities to fly with him and his wife to Hong Kong, six months before scheduled service was to be extended from Manila to the British colony. The party was greeted by crowds, flags, movie cameras, and a band. Trippe responded to the official speech of welcome, then turned over the microphone to the pilot of the S-42, Captain John Tilton.

"The parrot," said the captain, "is the only bird that can speak . . . and it's no damn good at flying."

Captain Tilton may have been tongue-tied, but, like his colleague Marius Lodeesen, he was undoubtedly well-read. The originator of this quip was none other than Wilbur Wright. The elder of the Wright brothers had been pressed to "say a few words" at the end of a dinner of a French aeronautical society in 1908. The only difference was that Wright, the bishop's son, described the parrot as "rather poor at flying."

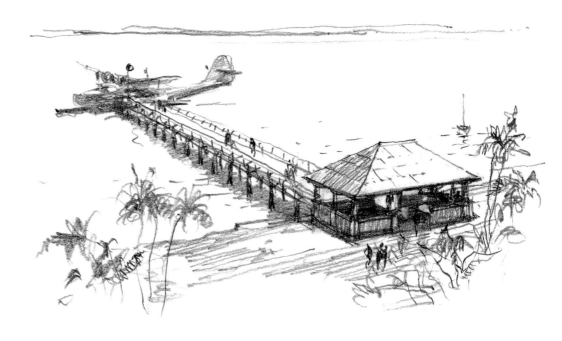

The Clipper dock in the lagoon at Wake Island

PLATE 14.

Blériot 5190 Santos Dumont *at Rio de Janeiro, 1935*

In Rio of the 1930s, the complete man-about-town would have his house in Gavea, belong to the Jockey Club, and drive a Delage with custom-built coachwork by Saoutchik. His wife would keep a poodle and have her Paris hats delivered by air.

Named for the Brazilian pioneer of powered flight, who carried out his work in Paris before returning to his homeland in 1906, this French mailplane has an exotic appearance suggestive of a modern nuclear submarine.

In 1928, a French businessman, Marcel Bouilloux-Lafont, started an air-mail service from Paris to Rio and Buenos Aires, making use of ships to complete the South Atlantic crossing. In 1930, his airline, called Aeropostale, employed a Latécoère 28 floatplane to make the direct crossing from Senegal to Natal, in Brazil. The pilot was the celebrated Jean Mermoz, who became a national hero for this and other aerial feats. Within a year this company was forced into liquidation.

In 1930, the French government placed orders for one model each of two types of long range multi-engined flying boats to perform mail service across the South Atlantic. The first was the Latécoère 300, which was named *Croix du Sud* (see plate number eight), and the second was the Blériot 5190, named *Santos Dumont*. The Laté was powered by four twelve-cylinder watercooled engines made by Hispano-Suiza, mounted back-to-back above the wings in two nacelles. Her top speed was 100 mph but her load capacity was just about equal to the weight of the airframe, which enabled her to carry sufficient fuel to make a record-breaking flight of 2,300 miles (without payload) in 1933. Three more aircraft of the type were built for Air France, and two of them continued in service carrying mail to Brazil and Argentina until 1940. The original *Croix du Sud* was lost at sea in December 1936, with Jean Mermoz at the controls.

The Blériot had four similar engines, but they were arranged with three pulling and only one pushing. They had the advantage of being fitted with variable-pitch propellers. The aircraft, however, was delayed in production and she made her first transatlantic flight in November 1934, some twelve months later than the Laté. The Blériot lacked the load capacity and thus the range of her compatriot, but she could cruise at 118 mph over a distance of up to 2,000 miles. *Santos Dumont* made thirty Atlantic crossings, but her service life was short and she was retired earlier than the Laté 300. If she had been employed on Mediterranean routes, she was reckoned to be capable of carrying up to forty passengers.

PLATE 15.

Sikorsky S-42A Jamaica Clipper, *background Pão de Açúcar,*
  Rio de Janeiro, 1936

The Sikorsky S-42 first went into service on Pan American's Caribbean and South American routes. Introduced in 1934, soon after the DC-2, which was widely used by airlines operating within the US, the flying boat had twice the range and three times the carrying capacity of the landplane.

The S-42A, second variant of the type, had slightly more powerful engines which gave her a cruising speed of 160 mph and a maximum range of 1,200 miles. The boat could accommodate up to a total of thirty-two passengers over a range of 750 miles, depending on conditions. A later variant, the S-42B, could achieve flights of 1,800 miles or more.

Entry was by means of sliding hatches in the flat central section on top of the fuselage, which avoided the possible weakness of water penetrating through doorways cut into the side of the hull. All sorts of stories were told about experiences with the S-42, because the plane was breaking new ground in many directions. One concerned the "heads," or lavatories: common practice of the day was simply to discharge effluent in flight. The aerodynamics of the S-42 were such as to cause an updraft in certain circumstances, and interrupted crew members devised a warning notice which read: "Not to be used when plane is in motion."

Flying boats landed in Guanabara Bay, on the west side of which lies the city of Rio. The famous Santos Dumont Airport was built on reclaimed land close to the city center. The entrance to the bay is marked by the well-known landmark of Pão de Açúcar (Sugar Loaf) mountain, which could present an obstruction to takeoffs from within the bay. In the painting, *Jamaica Clipper* has elected to taxi close to the mountain to ensure a clear run back towards the north.

PLATE 16.

Short S 17 Kents and Short S 8 Calcuttas moored off Hythe in Southampton Water, 1936

The flying boat maintenance base of Imperial Airways was at Hythe, a village on the western shore of Southampton Water, downstream from the confluence of the River Itchen with the Test, between which lies the city of Southampton and its docks.

This dawn view shows almost the entire company fleet of rather elderly-looking flying boats, shortly before the spanking new S 23 "Empire" boats started to take over in October 1936.

In the background, the new mailship *Athlone Castle* of the Union Castle Line is leaving the docks and heading towards the Solent.

The Calcutta was a three-engined type developed from the Singapore 1, a military plane, one of which had been used by Sir Alan Cobham on his survey flight throughout Africa. Five Calcuttas were built for Imperial Airways, delivered in 1928 and 1929, and the French government bought one more. They carried fifteen passengers at ninety mph over a maximum distance of 650 miles and were used on the Mediterranean segment of the empire routes.

The Short S 17 Kent was a four-engined aircraft with a more spacious passenger cabin than the Calcutta; three of them were added to the fleet in 1931.

Imperial Airways' Calcuttas were named *City of Alexandria, City of Athens, City of Rome, City of Khartoum,* and *City of Swanage.* The Kents were called *Scipio, Sylvanus,* and *Satyrus.*

The Imperial Airways terminal in London had direct rail access to Southampton

PLATE 17.

Sikorsky S-43s of Panair do Brasil at Rio de Janeiro, 1936

The "Baby Clipper," as she was called, was a scaled-down version of the four-engined S-42. This amphibian flying boat was similar in layout but had two Pratt & Whitney Hornet engines in place of four. The S-43 could take eighteen passengers and had an operating range of about 750 miles. Some examples of the S-43 were built with twin tail fins.

Thirteen S-43s were ordered by Pan American, and delivery started in January 1936. Seven of the aircraft were allocated to its Brazilian affiliate, Panair do Brasil. Two went to Pan American-Grace Airways (Panagra) for service on the west coast of South America, and the remainder flew on Pan American's Caribbean network.

Two Baby Clippers are shown here at Rio's Santos Dumont Airport, which is built on a landfill jutting out into Guanabara Bay. In the background can be seen the battleship *Sao Paulo*, lying at moorings off the naval base on Ilha das Cobras, and a car-ferry which is on its way across the bay to Niteroi. Note the flight of cormorants, a familiar sight over these waters.

In 1936, Pan American visualized starting a flying boat service from Copenhagen to Reykjavik in Iceland, in collaboration with a Danish airline. The intention was to extend the route by 1938 all the way to the US. Sikorsky S-43s were to be used for this operation, but the project never materialized. Intermediate stops would have been made in the Shetlands and the Faroe Islands, as well as in Greenland and at other points in North America.

Sikorsky S-43, the Baby Clipper, alongside a dock

PLATE 18.

Short S 23 "Empire" flying boat taking off at Rod-El-Farag, Cairo, 1936

Rod-El-Farag, on the right bank downriver from central Cairo, was the junction of Imperial's services to the Middle East, India, the Far East, and Australia with the African route which followed the Nile up to Lake Victoria and thence down the east coast to Durban. The houseboat *Mayflower* was moored to the bank to serve passengers as a rest house. Observe the windsock which is hoisted on the steamer. Twelve years later I was a passenger in a Hunting Clan Viscount which made an overnight stop at Wadi Halfa; we were accommodated, as I remember it, in a more modest Nile steamer.

"Empire" boats were fitted with sleeping berths which were used on those flights which included overnight stages, and many of the civilities of sea travel were maintained by Imperial Airways. On boarding, passengers received a gold-edged card engraved with their name, together with a thirty-page booklet describing the sights along the route. Writing paper was provided, embossed with the name of the individual aircraft, its badge, and an epigram. On crossing the equator, initiates were presented with a decorative manuscript inscribed by King Neptune himself to commemorate the occasion. The intimate character of flying boat travel was largely due to the initiative of individual stewards. One passenger recalled that during the holiday season, a Christmas tree was set up on the promenade deck, and the chief steward distributed tiny gift-wrapped packages, the contents of which were stamped with the initials of each passenger.

The interiors of the "Empire" boats belonged to the age of green leather seats, decorative hardwood veneers, and linen curtains. Pursers would contrive to have bowls of fresh-cut flowers on the dining tables, at least for the start of a trip.

A single crew would man the aircraft for the whole journey of a week or more, which partly accounts for schedules including many overnight stops. The captain would stroll through the cabins to introduce himself to passengers, and it was common to invite visitors to the flight deck. Nobody, in those days, imagined the possibility of an airplane being hijacked.

Steward serving early morning tea to sleeping-berth passengers in an "Empire" boat

PLATE 19.

Martin M-130 Hawaiian Clipper *over the incomplete* Golden Gate Bridge, San Francisco, 1936

The M-130 had the range to make the first leap in Pan Am's island-hopping route from San Francisco to the Orient. The margin was not great. Before takeoff, the first task was to calculate the load of fuel which would be required for the flight that day, depending on the meteorological forecast, then to ascertain the weight of mail that had to be carried, for the mail contract received priority. Only after that was the captain able to work out the number of passengers that could be accommodated. Generally it was six to eight, and they could therefore be notified only on the morning of departure. Average loads to Honolulu, in fact, seldom exceeded half that number, partly because of the high fare.

Mail service was inaugurated by *China Clipper,* the first M-130, in November 1935, but the first scheduled passenger flight was not until eleven months later. The second boat, *Hawaiian Clipper,* is seen here on her way with passengers to Honolulu in October 1936, six months before the Golden Gate Bridge reached completion. The third ship of the three ordered by Pan Am was named *Philippine Clipper.* The orange stripe painted on the top surface of the wing was intended to assist search and rescue operations in the event of the flying boat being forced down in the sea.

Ford V8 station wagon at Midway

The M-130s were larger and sleeker than the Sikorsky S-42s. They were a little slower but they had a longer range. Each M-130 cost $417,000, compared to $242,000 for an S-42 or $78,000 for a Douglas DC-2 twin-engined landplane, which had only a quarter of the range. The fare from San Francisco to Manila (one-way) was $777, the price of a new Plymouth automobile at the time.

PLATE 20.

Sikorsky S–42B Samoan Clipper *at Pago Pago, American Samoa, 1937*

In March 1937, Captain Ed Musick flew Pan American's *Samoan Clipper* on the first survey flight from Honolulu to Auckland, New Zealand. Stops were made at Kingman Reef and at Pago Pago in American Samoa. Kingman Reef was an uninhabited islet no more than 120 feet long which rose barely three feet above the sea. To make it a practicable refueling base it was necessary to station there a ship carrying gasoline and equipped with radio direction-finding gear. Pago Pago was a sheltered harbor, but it was almost surrounded by 1,500-foot-high hills which dropped steeply to the water. For landing and take-off, it was distinctly hazardous.

On the outbound flight, the Sikorsky suffered engine trouble which led the captain to decide to jettison fuel. Alarmingly, there were signs that some of the dumped gas had in some way been sucked into the plane. Windows were opened, electrical circuits other than those needed for the engines were shut down, and the airplane reached base safely.

Ed Musick found the harbor at Samoa even worse than he had been advised. The harbor mouth was roiled with combers kicked up by the tradewind, curtailing the possibility of any overrun when landing. It was, he said, "like trying to land in a teacup."

The outbound flight went on to reach Auckland safely, and the crew received a rapturous welcome from New Zealanders, who were happy that Pan American chose to make its destination with the Kiwis before the Koalas.

On his third trip to New Zealand, Musick again experienced engine trouble. Two hours out from Pago Pago, he radioed that he was returning, and that he intended to dump fuel before landing. The S-42 never made it. The accident investigation concluded that in dumping the fuel, gas vapors had collected inside part of the wings. Then an electrical spark, possibly generated by the flap motor, had ignited the vapor, and the aircraft had been destroyed by the resulting explosion.

André Priester, chief engineer of Pan Am, used to say that "the air, like the sea, is not inherently dangerous, but it is terribly unforgiving of incapacity or neglect."

The use of Pago Pago was abandoned, and when New Zealand flights started again with the Boeing Clippers in 1940, they were routed via Canton Island and Noumea, New Caledonia.

PLATE 21.

Short S 23 "Empire" boat **Capella** *just at splash-down*
on Lake Naivasha, Kenya, 1937

RMA *Capella* is depicted in this painting just at the moment of hitting the water as she alights on the glassy surface of the lake, which is full of reflections of tropical clouds and sky. In the distance lies the scarred cone of the dormant volcano called Mount Longonot.

The last and the smallest wave of farmer-settlers from Europe, who colonized seemingly under-utilized parts of the world, were those who set out after the Great War of 1914-18 to make a new life in Kenya. Between about 1900 and 1930, a few thousand settled in the lovely Highlands of East Africa, then almost empty of people. They succeeded, after an arduous struggle, in creating a viable agricultural industry in an ecological environment (more than 5,500 feet above sea level and on the equator) unlike any which had previously been brought under commercial cultivation.

The richly productive farmlands which are now to be found from Kiambu to Eldoret, and from Nanyuki to Kericho, are the outcome of that burst of enterprise. Settlers contributed substantially to the launch of a modern multicultural nation with a rather well-developed commercial and industrial sector, and with a healthy endowment of public services.

Flying boats landing on Lake Naivasha in the 1930s were very much part of this scene. They brought mail, family members, and colonial civil servants to the very midst of the farming country. Naivasha lies in the Great Rift Valley, with the highlands of the Mau Escarpment to the west and the Aberdares to the east. Forest, pasture, and arable land equal to the most beautiful in the world occupy the slopes on both sides.

Armstrong-Siddeley landaulette

70

PLATE 22.

Dornier Do 18 flying boat and Blohm & Voss Ha 139 floatplane at Horta, Azores, 1937

The color yellow has long been associated with mail coaches and buses in Europe. Driving a car in Switzerland, one needs to know that the yellow mail bus has priority on the inside track of hairpin bends, whether right or left, on a mountain road.

The yellow-painted Dornier Do 18 mailplane in the watercolor has just flown in to Horta, capital of the Azores Islands, from Lisbon. There she picked up the mail from Berlin, relayed to Portugal by landplanes. At Horta, the mailbags were transferred to a four-engined Blohm & Voss Ha 139 floatplane which, launched by catapult from the depot ship *Schwabenland*, flew direct to Long Island Sound, New York. Three of the floatplanes, *Nordwind*, *Nordmeer*, and *Nordstern*, made between them thirteen round trips in 1938.

The Do 18 was a graceful flying boat powered by two Junkers Jumo six-cylinder diesel engines which produced 880 hp. Her operational range was about 2,000 miles, with very limited payload. The Ha 139 floatplane, possibly the largest floatplane ever built, had four twelve-cylinder diesels, and had substantially greater speed and range than her compatriot. Her record crossing was made at an average speed of 173 mph over a distance of 2,400 miles.

Takeoff of the twelve-motor Dornier Do X was described as "an amazing spectacle"

The pilot of the Blohm & Voss floatplane undertook the grueling routine of maintaining altitude low above water level for many hours after launching, deriving some range advantage by exploiting "ground effect," and also delaying his climb until part of the heavy fuel load had been consumed.

PLATE 23.

Dornier Do J II Wal being catapulted from SS Westfallen, *with Dornier Do 26 overhead, 1938*

The Dornier Wal, which first entered service in 1924, seems to have been commercially the most successful flying boat before the Second World War. Some 300 Wals were built, plus twenty Super Wals. They were used in services across the Baltic and the Mediterranean, in Colombia, Brazil, China, and Japan. Because of postwar treaty restrictions, they were first made in Italy, Spain, Japan, and the Netherlands; only after 1932 was the Wal manufactured in its native Germany.

Wolfgang von Gronau, head of the German civil aviation school, used a Wal to make crossings of the North Atlantic in 1930 and the two successive years. He flew from the Baltic by the northern route via Iceland, Greenland, and Canada, and on the third occasion he continued around the world.

In 1934, Deutsche Lufthansa started a mail service between Berlin and Buenos Aires. The journey comprised fifteen sectors, most of them operated by landplanes, but flying boats were used for the South Atlantic crossing. During the first year, twenty-three round trips were accomplished, and by the outbreak of war in 1939 the total had reached 240. Do J II Wals were employed on the overwater sectors, launched by catapult from depot ships in order to increase their range.

One ship was stationed off the coast near Bathurst in Gambia, West Africa, and another near Natal on the easternmost tip of Brazil. After a short flight from land, the flying boat alighted close to the ship. The plane would taxi up to the stern and onto a mat, or "drag-sail," towed on the surface, before being hoisted aboard by crane. This was to reduce the undulations of waves and ocean swell. Launching by catapult enabled the aircraft to become airborne with a much heavier load of fuel than when taking off under its own power.

The Dornier Do 26 was the most streamlined of all flying boats

The first of the catapult ships, a converted freighter called *Westfallen*, was soon joined by the *Schwabenland*. In 1936, a smaller but more capable vessel, *Ostmark*, was introduced, followed a year later by a larger, purpose-built depot ship named *Friesenland*.

The Do 26, seen in this picture flying low towards the launching ship, was a much enlarged and improved type of flying boat. It was designed to achieve the increased range required for North Atlantic mail service. This sleek aircraft had retractable wingtip floats and a speed of over 200 mph. Four liquid-cooled diesel engines were mounted in tandem in two nacelles, the rear engines driven through shafts which could be tilted ten degrees upwards to clear the propellers from spray during takeoff and landing. Two airplanes of this type were employed on the South Atlantic for a few weeks in 1938, but they were never put into regular service.

I. H. M.

PLATE 24.

Short-Mayo S 20 **Mercury** *floatplane immediately after disengagement from Short S 21* **Maia** *flying boat, 1938*

The notion of launching planes at cruising altitude was not, perhaps, as dotty as it may appear. A substantial portion of the available fuel load is consumed in takeoff and climb. Airlines pushing to extend range and payload were driven to explore such methods, while calling for engine manufacturers to produce ever more powerful and economical engines.

It was in 1916 that John Porte experimented with composite aircraft, a flying boat being employed to lift a small scout plane to operating height. Major Mayo of Imperial Airways developed the idea from 1932, but took a long time to persuade the Air Ministry to contribute towards its construction. For transatlantic operation, the airline wanted to build half-a-dozen small, long-range mailplanes which would be launched at altitude by a flying boat. A four-engined floatplane to Mayo's design was eventually produced in 1938. A flying boat had been constructed during this period to act as launching platform, and the composite was successfully flown in 1938. The design of this flying boat, with few changes, evolved into that of the "Empire" boats.

In July of that year, *Mercury* was launched by *Maia* over the Shannon River in Ireland, and flew direct to Montreal with 2,200 pounds of mail. The floatplane had to return by shorter stages. The airline was keen to follow up this initiative with more mailplanes and regular operation, but the Air Ministry rightly decided that there was no future in a purely airmail project.

Mercury was launched by *Maia* on two flights to Alexandria later in 1938, carrying Christmas mail, but this was the end of the experiment. There is a photograph of mailbags being stuffed through a small hatch into one of *Mercury*'s floats. Airline officials had touching faith that there would be no leaks.

Mercury, in mythology, suggests "winged messenger."

PLATE 25.

Sikorsky S-42A Antilles Clipper *landing at Dinner Key, Miami, 1938*

The Sikorsky S-42 seems to have been known to everyone in the airline business as the Betsy. I asked each person I met how she came to be given that name, and no one could provide the answer. Finally, I heard it from John Borger, one-time chief engineer of the Atlantic Division of Pan American. It seems that she was named by a captain called Lou Lindsey. "She's a real Betsy," he said, "like a mare in heat, she carries her tail up high and waggles her rump."

Ten S-42s were built for Pan Am, and at first they operated out of the base at Dinner Key in Biscayne Bay, Miami. The island's name derived from its being a popular destination for boating picnics, but in 1930 the airline bought it to create a marine air terminal for services to the Caribbean and Latin America. The island was linked by fill to the mainland, hangars and ramps were built for seaplanes, and a smart "modernistic" style passenger terminal was constructed as the centerpiece.

During the Second World War, airfields were built for defense throughout the Caribbean, South America, and Central America. With the end of the war in 1945, landplanes were released from military service and Pan American re-placed its flying boats with DC-4s and Constellations. The marine air terminal was closed, and in 1946 Dinner Key was sold. The passenger terminal, with its decorative frieze incorporating the Pan Am winged globe emblem, was turned into Miami City Hall, and the handsome art deco building is maintained in immaculate condition by the city council. A bronze plaque facing the entrance proudly records the flying boat story.

Packard convertible coupé

PLATE 26.

Short S 23 "Empire" boat Coriolanus *from the rest house verandah at Koepang, Timor, 1938*

The first "Empire" boats from England, *Camilla* and *Capella*, arrived at Rose Bay, Sydney, in July 1938. Shortly afterwards, flights were extended across the Tasman Sea to Auckland in New Zealand.

A tripartite company called Tasman Empire Airways was set up jointly by Britain, New Zealand, and Australia to bring service to New Zealand, and five "Empire" flying boats were ordered. Before the war began, two of them entered service and were given Maori names. The Australian airline Qantas operated six more aircraft of the same type.

The "Empire" boats had an operating range of about 800 miles, less than that of contemporary American types, but they were designed for trade routes that did not involve ocean crossings. Later boats in the series had an extended range. A larger variant of the type, the S 26 (G-class), was built in 1939 with the intention of operating across the North Atlantic.

The Short flying boats were furnished to seat twenty-four passengers by day or nineteen in bunks for overnight travel. The demand for mail was so heavy that more than 4,000 pounds was generally carried per flight, so that passenger accommodation was later reduced to a maximum of seventeen. On occasions, the mail load was up to 10,000 pounds, or the equivalent of fifty passengers.

With a cruising speed of about 165 mph, the aircraft were fast for their day and they were comfortably equipped for passengers, but they did not score high in economic efficiency. The load to tare ratio was 25 : 75, compared to the Sikorsky S-42's figure of 42 : 58.

Mooring an "Empire" boat at Sharjah

Imperial Airways missed a personality with the rigorous professionalism of Pan Am's André Priester. The British seem to have left more responsibility, and more discretion, in the hands of individual captains. Imperial's route system was enormously spread out compared to Pan American's, and operating conditions were extremely diverse. With the rapid commissioning of twenty-eight flying boats, flying to more than fifty destinations scattered in different countries, there was an unfortunate series of accidents. The loss of life was not large, but during the three years of operation before the outbreak of war, eight aircraft were either destroyed or so badly damaged in accidents that they had to be written-off.

PLATE 27.

Short S 23 "Empire" boat **Calypso** *at Mombasa, Kenya, 1938*

The Imperial Airways flying boat is taxiing amongst steamers tied up alongside the docks at Kilindini, with Port Reitz in the background. Two of the ships are painted in the smart black and white livery of the British India Line. Mombasa seems to be anticipating a typical afternoon downpour during the northeast monsoon.

Mombasa was the first port-of-call for Imperial Airways on the Indian Ocean, after following the River Nile for almost all its lengh to Lake Victoria, and thence overland across Kenya.

Similar scenes were enacted at several other ports down the coast of East Africa, such as Dar es Salaam, Beira, Lourenço Marques, and Durban. The "Empire" boats had to be nippy to get into and out of such restricted harbors, which were busy with shipping and small craft.

The S 23 was powered by four Bristol Pegasus X nine-cylinder air-cooled engines of 910 hp, which gave it a cruising speed of 165 mph. The later S 30 version had Bristol Perseus XII engines, which conferred considerably greater range. A total of forty-two aircraft of the two types were built, and they remained in service from 1936 to 1947, though numbers were much depleted by accidents and by war losses. They flew altogether thirty-eight million miles in commercial service.

A smart Pan Am passenger tender

Imperial Airways "control launch" designed by Hubert Scott-Paine, who was also largely responsible for the Motor Torpedo Boat type used by the Royal Navy and the US Navy's PT Boat design. The launches were built by the British Power Boat Co. of Hythe, on Southampton Water.

PLATE 28.

Sikorsky S–42B Bermuda Clipper *landing on the Great Sound, Bermuda, 1939*

In June 1937, Pan American and Imperial Airways started a joint service between New York and Bermuda. Pan Am used *Bermuda Clipper,* a Sikorsky S-42B, while Imperial used *Cavalier,* a Short S 23 "Empire" boat. They flew twice a week between Port Washington on the shore of Long Island Sound, and Darrell's Island, in the Great Sound near Hamilton, Bermuda. The distance was about 700 miles and each plane took six hours. The last four S-42 aircraft built were designated S-42B; they were equipped with Hamilton "constant-speed" propellers which delivered a marked improvement in efficiency.

Pan American engineers were always finding room for improvements to their airplanes, and one of the relatively less serious defects was the difficulty of opening the sliding door to the toilet compartment. The toilet was located between the flight deck and the forward end of the passenger compartment, and the aluminum door frequently jammed on its sliding track. On one Bermuda trip, the flight engineer made his way to the toilet but could not persuade the door to slide open. He returned to his work station and brought back a small toolkit, which enabled him to unscrew the offending door from its overhead sliding gear and to stow it carefully on one side. He was startled, however, to be addressed by a little old lady who was occupying the throne: "Young man, you can just put back every single one of those screws and tighten them up again. I shall let you know when I'm finished." The chastened engineer complied, and then beat a retreat to the flight deck.

Next day, just before *Bermuda Clipper* was about to cast off, the passenger launch from Hamilton hove into sight. On board was a messenger with a parcel addressed to the flight engineer. Inside was a gift-wrapped box containing "the very best screwdriver that the hardware stores on the Island have to offer."

The end of the Imperial service was a sorry one, for in January 1939, *Cavalier* was lost in an accident that cost the lives of three out of thirteen people on board. The airplane ran into bad weather which caused two engines to shut down and the remaining two to start to fail. The cause was carburetor icing, which was not a new problem, and one which Pan Am had been able to overcome. Imperial had failed to take measures to avoid it, and after landing in heavy seas the Short S 23 began to break up before a rescue ship reached the scene.

Passengers enjoyed rather good vision from the cabin of an S-42

PLATE 29.

Martin M-130 Philippine Clipper *at Treasure Island Marine Air Terminal, San Francisco Bay, 1939*

The sponson, or "sea wing," of this Martin M-130 provides a convenient platform for ground crew engaged in maintenance operations. Several aircraft types of the era incorporated ribbed areas of duralumin sheeting to confer additional rigidity to their stressed skin construction.

In the background can be seen part of the Oakland Bay Bridge where it reaches Yerba Buena Island, midway between Oakland and San Francisco. The long suspension bridge between the island and San Francisco was incomplete when the *China Clipper* left from nearby Alameda, carrying the first transpacific airmail to Manila, on 22 November 1935. The pilot, Ed Musick, found himself unable to climb quickly enough after leaving the water, so he took the flying boat under the cables of one of the two main spans. The road deck had not yet been constructed. Reporters covering the occasion supposed, erroneously, that this was a piece of showmanship.

It was necessary to check the calibration of an aircraft's airspeed indicator from time to time. This was done by flying over two of the bridges in San Francisco Bay. Runs would be made at 200 feet altitude at four or five speeds, and the recorded times compared with measured distances between the bridges. Economical cruising was dependent on careful adjustment of height and speed depending on wind conditions; the most economical speed was also affected by the steadily diminishing weight as fuel was consumed.

The M-130 was fitted initially with four Pratt & Whitney Twin Wasp engines of 830 hp, later to be replaced by engines rated at 950 hp and with "constant-speed" (automatically variable-pitch) propellers. Cruising speed was 130 mph and operating range was about 2,500 miles, depending on payload and wind direction.

The Manila Hotel, Manila, Philippines

PLATE 30.

Short S 23 "Empire" boat **Cassiopeia** *boarding passengers at Luxor, 1939*

In the 1930s, air travel was more arduous as well as slower than it is today, and with unpressurized aircraft it was much noisier and often more bumpy. There were, however, compensations. On Imperial Airways' "Empire" routes, there were opportunities for sightseeing along the way.

In recent times, the tourist industry—and in particular the cruise ship business—has exploited the fascination that most people have for exploring rather than merely traveling. If you took the Imperial flight up the Nile towards the great lakes of central Africa, your airplane touched down at Luxor (site of ancient Thebes), 100 miles downstream from the First Cataract at Aswan. There, you were accommodated by the airline at the Winter Palace Hotel. Time was found during the course of your stay to visit one or two at least of the temples at Luxor, Thebes, or Karnak, and the Valley of the Kings.

Next day, flying south across the tropic of Cancer, your "Empire" boat took a straight line over the Nubian Desert, leaving the Nile to meander far away to the west and then to the east. At Khartoum, the airplane alighted at a spot called Gordon's Tree, near the confluence of the Blue Nile with the White. And so it was all the way along the route: the S 23 flew low over great herds of game further south, and leisurely stops were made for refueling or for overnight stays.

Refueling about to take place at Gwadar

PLATE 31.

Boeing B-314 Honolulu Clipper *at Treasure Island, San Francisco Bay, 1939*

Boeing Clipper flying boat services were inaugurated on both coasts of the United States simultaneously with big-time fairs. In San Francisco, the Golden Gate International Exposition opened on Treasure Island in 1939, the same year when the big Boeings, built in Seattle, started to fly on the Pacific routes. On the East Coast, the 1939 World's Fair was held at Flushing Meadow, Long Island, New York. On May 20, a B-314 flew over the fairground to celebrate the start of the first transatlantic service. The flying boat took off from Port Washington on Manhasset Bay, Long Island, not far from the site of the World's Fair.

Pan Am decided to transfer its San Francisco base from Alameda, across from the Oakland waterfront, to Treasure Island, the site of the West Coast exposition. This artificial island had been created by landfill immediately north of Yerba Buena Island, midpoint of the Oakland Bay and San Francisco bridges. The flying boat operation and its terminal building were an integral part of the show. Seen here in the background is the Oakland Bay Bridge on the left, with the Matson Line steamer ss *Mariposa* lying at anchor. She and her sister ships *Lurline* and *Monterey* operated a mail service between Pacific coast ports and Australasia.

The B-314 was equipped with four Wright Double Cyclone radial engines that delivered 1200 hp, with "constant-speed" propellers. She had a cruising speed of 165 mph and the operating range seems to have been rather less than 3,000 miles, though more was often quoted. Later production models were fitted with more powerful Pratt & Whitney Double Wasp engines, and these were retrofitted to the first six aircraft. Accommodation was available for as many as seventy-four passengers, but between thirty and forty was typical on ocean crossings.

The Boeing Clippers were a major job to get out of the water

Saltwater corrosion was a perennial problem. Clippers were treated with black bitumastic paint on the bottom of the hull, and this in turn was coated with lanolin. In spite of these measures, some corrosion inevitably occurred, and the black coating tended to conceal it, so later practice was to use lanolin alone. The additional weight of the bitumastic material was also a significant factor in the decision to do without it. Interiors of sponsons had to be inspected for corrosion, which meant that a slim engineer was required to wriggle headfirst into this extraordinarily inaccessible space.

PLATE 32.

Consolidated PBY-2 Guba *at Diego Garcia in the Chagos Archipelago, with the cruiser HMS* Manchester, *1939*

One of the first PBYs off the production line was built for Dr. Richard Archbold of the New York Museum of Natural History. Delivered in 1937, it was intended for use in Dutch New Guinea and was named *Guba*. This first aircraft was rushed into use in a vain attempt to find a Russian party lost while attempting to fly over the North Pole, and was eventually sold to Russia. The second *Guba* reached New Guinea in June 1938.

Twelve months later, *Guba* was chartered by the Australian pioneer aviator Sir Gordon Taylor, with a view to surveying an air route across the Indian Ocean. The project received Australian and British government support, particularly because of the prospect of Australia becoming isolated in the event of the Japanese occupation of Singapore.

With a mixed Australian and American crew, Taylor and Archbold set off from Port Hedland in northwest Australia to fly to Cocos Island and thence to Diego Garcia, Mahé in the Seychelles Islands, and eventually to Mombasa, Kenya. Great difficulty was experienced in navigating without effective radio beacons, and on the first attempt to find Cocos Island, *Guba* had to divert to Batavia in Java. When she reached Diego Garcia, they were again faced with clouds, but eventually they spotted, through a break, the cruiser HMS *Manchester* lying at anchor to greet the flying boat on arrival.

Guba carried on across Africa, landing on Lake Victoria, at Coquilhatville on the River Congo, and at Dakar. She returned to New York via St. Thomas in the West Indies, and finally to San Diego in July 1939. This seems to have been the first aerial circumnavigation of the world at roughly the latitude of the equator.

A great many PBYs were bought by Britain for use by the RAF, which gave them the name Catalina. *Guba* herself was among the aircraft purchased. When the Japanese occupied Malaya and then the Dutch East Indies early in 1942, the Indian Ocean air route indeed became a matter of vital importance to Australia. Catalinas were used to maintain communications, and from June 1943 the Australian airline Qantas flew a regular service between Trincomalee in Ceylon and Exmouth Bay in northwest Australia, a distance of more than 2,600 miles. There was a possible refueling stop at Cocos Island, depending on enemy activity and weather conditions, but the route was an extraordinary feat of airmanship in its day.

Qantas continued to use Catalinas in scheduled service until 1958, and other non-US PBYs were used by Air France, KLM, Cathay Pacific, Thai Airways, Trans-Australian, and Bahamasair.

PLATE 33.

Short S 23 "Empire" boat **Ceres** *boarding passengers
at Laropi on the Albert Nile, Uganda, 1939*

Boarding a flying boat on the British Empire routes could be a little tricky. Imperial Airways employed what they called "control launches," which were stationed at all stopping points. A total of sixty were supplied by the British Power Boat Company. They were thirty-seven feet long, painted in the airline livery of indigo blue and white, and they were always immaculately kept and smartly handled. Launches were used for passenger transfers, to clear and inspect landing areas, tend to moorings, light flares, and place marker buoys when needed. Other tenders were equipped for refueling and maintenance of aircraft. Curiously, control launches, tenders, and moorings were all under the ultimate control of the Admiralty. Turf was guarded jealously in Whitehall, and memories were long.

Passengers disembarking at a place such as Laropi, in northern Uganda, would find themselves abruptly in very primitive surroundings indeed. In these days of universal immigration and customs formalities, duty-free shops, car rental desks and airline check-in counters, it is hard to imagine how it must have been to step off a flying boat in Laropi in 1939. The world's most modern aircraft carried you from London to a remote spot which today is far less accessible, and which offered absolutely no conveniences to cushion the cultural shock. There are a few people still alive who experienced that adventurous way of arrival.

The "Empire" boats were capable of putting down on very restricted bodies of water. They landed at such out-of-the-way places as Wadi Halfa, Malakal, and Juba on the Nile; Port Bell and Kisumu on Lake Victoria; Mombasa, Dar es Salaam and Lindi, on the coast of British East Africa; Lumba (for Mozambique Island), Beira, and Quelimane in Portuguese East Africa. During the war years they operated through Coquilhatville and Stanleyville in the Belgian Congo.

PLATE 34.

Boeing B-314 **Dixie Clipper** *loading passengers at Port Washington, Long Island, New York, 1939*

Dixie Clipper inaugurated the first transatlantic airplane passenger service on 28 June 1939. She left the dock at Pan American's Port Washington terminal in Manhasset Bay, Long Island Sound, with twenty-two passengers on board. The flight operated from New York to Lisbon and Marseilles, via Horta in the Azores. At the time, there was no such thing as a pressurized aircraft. On the first flight, Betty Trippe noted that at 8,000 feet the stewards found it strenuous work to make up the bunks, and she advised her husband, the president of the airline, that more blankets were needed to combat the cold.

To our eyes, the aircraft looks bloated, but in its day the Boeing Clipper appeared impressively sleek and streamlined, and it seemed immense. It was larger than any operational aircraft of the time, and it had accommodation for up to seventy-four passengers plus a crew of twelve. It had a separate dining room, there were berths for forty people overnight, separate dressing rooms and toilets for men and women, and in the tail of the fuselage was located the honeymoon suite. Henry Spenceley, booking clerk for Pan Am in New York, found himself in trouble with the Portuguese authorities on account of two ostensible "honeymooners." It seems he booked two people into the double-bedded suite at the tail of the plane without checking their passports. On arrival in Lisbon, officials were horrified to discover that an unmarried couple had made the transatlantic crossing in such fashion. The *responsable* found himself in very hot water.

In common with most civil aircraft of the day, Pan American Clippers were unpainted duralumin or silver in color. The airline name and insignia were painted in very dark blue. With the looming prospect of war in Europe,

Looking aft through the main lounge of a B-314

in late August of 1939 the national flag was painted boldly on both sides of the planes at the bow. The British followed suit with their own civilian airliners.

One interesting detail of construction was that the wings were thick enough to permit a crawlspace, entered from the flight deck, penetrating through one rib after another to permit access to the engines in flight. Only very limited operations could be performed on the rear of the engines, but accessibility did prove useful on occasion, not least—while the aircraft was docked—for a four-handed poker game. Juan Trippe recognized the publicity value of this safety feature and made much of it in speeches.

PLATE 35.

Latécoère 522 Ville de Saint Pierre *overflying SS* Normandie, *July 30, 1939*

Designed as a North Atlantic flier, the Laté 521 first took to the air in January 1935. Even though she was powered by six 890 hp V12 Hispano-Suiza engines, this proved insufficient both in power and reliability to carry out the intention of scheduled transatlantic flights with a payload of thirty passengers. The first aircraft of the type, *Lieutenant de Vaisseau Paris*, nevertheless crossed from Africa to Brazil and up to the United States in December 1935, before she was almost destroyed by a hurricane in Pensacola, Florida. The airplane was rebuilt in France, and in 1939 she was joined by a second, equipped with more powerful engines. Both flying boats made crossings of the North Atlantic via Foynes and Botwood, as well as by way of the Azores and Bermuda, but they were not yet ready to begin commercial service.

On one flight, Laté 522 *Ville de Saint Pierre* flew low over and saluted her namesake, the tiny French island of Saint Pierre, which lies with Miquelon close to the south coast of Newfoundland. She also managed to arrange an ocean rendezvous with the pride of the French Atlantic Line, the resplendent liner ss *Normandie*.

The 522's engine layout was unusual. Six engines were mounted in four nacelles, two of which contained engines in tandem, one pusher and one tractor back-to-back.

Latécoère 581 six-motor two-decker of 1938

PLATE 36.

Short S 30 "Empire" boat Cabot at Berth 108, Southampton, 1939

The British treated their flying boats as ships, and at Southampton, as well as at other ports, the airliners landed amongst shipping and tied up alongside jetties with other ocean liners. Their captains had to pass exams in seamanship, and they had to acquire the skills of navigation and mooring in busy waters, complicated sometimes by contrary conditions of wind and tide.

For maintenance, the flying boats tied up at their mooring buoys off Hythe, on the southwest side of Southampton Water. At different periods there were floating jetties for aircraft at Berth 108, at the north end of the New Docks, at Berth 101, and at Berth 50, between Town Quay and the Old Docks, close to Canute Road. Imperial Airways built a Modern Movement terminal building alongside Berth 108, which was served directly by rail from Victoria Air Terminal in London, but during the war flying boat operations were moved for safety to the shallow waters of Poole Harbour, twenty miles to the west. Southampton suffered very heavily from bombing and this terminal was destroyed.

Cabot was one of the S 30 boats, with longer range than that of the S 23s, and she was equipped for aerial refueling. She and her sister ship *Caribou* operated a transatlantic mail service from Southampton to Montreal from 8 August 1939 until October of that year, a few weeks after the outbreak of war. They were refueled in the air over Ireland on the westbound crossing and over Newfoundland on the return.

Cabot is flying two flags, the Civil Air Ensign and the Royal Air Mail Pennant. The routine was to raise flags on a short staff above the cockpit, after landing, and to recover them before takeoff. The Air Ensign was established in 1931 by order of King George V and the Royal Air Mail Pennant (dark blue background instead of white, as on ships) was granted in 1934. Imperial Airways also possessed a House Flag, resembling a yacht club burgee, but this seldom seems to have been used. In foreign ports, the national flag of the host country was flown on a short staff corresponding to the one supporting the mail pennant, the ensign being mounted above the wireless mast and therefore higher. In the 1950s, it was commonplace to spot little national flags fluttering above the cockpits of airliners at Heathrow Airport. It is a pity that they are no more.

In the background is the Canadian Pacific liner *Empress of Australia*, and in the distance can be seen the funnels of the *Queen Mary*.

Pullman car Lydia *boarding Imperial passengers for London*

PLATE 37.

Boeing B-314 taking off from Bowery Bay, off New York's La Guardia Marine Air Terminal, 1940

The Boeing Clipper is shown here "running on the step," just before lifting off the water. Flying boat hulls were designed to allow the aircraft to plane after achieving a certain speed, only the forward part remaining in contact with water. This reduced the area subject to water resistance, enabling the boat to continue to accelerate until it gained sufficient lift to break the remaining surface tension and become airborne. The standard arrangement was a two-step hull, but the devil lay in the details.

The big Boeings were tricky to handle in the water. Until Pan American Airways insisted on improvements, the boats were inclined to "porpoise"— that is, to pitch lengthwise. Tests were made in a ship model tank and eventually the problem was solved by extending the first step aft by an additional twenty-three inches.

Pan Am Marine Air Terminal at La Guardia, which is now used by the Delta Shuttle

Takeoff runs were seriously affected by surface water conditions, as well as by wind speed, load and power. Experienced passengers would carefully time the run: the FAA called for an average of no more than sixty seconds. The S-42 could usually get airborne in forty-five seconds, but the Martin and the Boeing were known to take over a minute in choppy conditions.

The Martin Company introduced what it called "seawings" to take the place of wingtip floats for stabilizing aircraft in the water, and a similar device was adopted by Boeing. They were aerodynamically cleaner than wingtip floats, and arguably they added some lift. Both manufacturers designed them to double as fuel tanks. Seawings were otherwise described as sponsons, or hydro-stabilizers. On the Boeings, it was found that they became ineffective above a certain speed, when a trough created by the bow wave left them clear of the water. Sponsons on the big Boeings performed a third useful function as platforms for passenger embarkation. In Liberia, West Africa, during the Second World War, the crews found out that it was wise to shoo off any crocodiles before trying to board the aircraft. The creatures regarded sponsons as convenient spots for sunbathing.

Such an inconvenience was rare in Bowery Bay. Visible in the distance is Hell Gate Bridge, which carries the tracks connecting the New Haven with the Long Island Railroad across the Narrows. Today, Amtrak trains from Boston use this route to reach Brooklyn before running in a tunnel under the East River and into Penn Station.

Pan American's circular art deco Marine Air Terminal building at La Guardia was opened in March 1940. It was designed by architects Delano and Aldrich and the centerpiece was a globe, reflecting the airline's insignia. The surrounding heroic mural has recently been restored, together with a charming frieze, incorporating blue and gold flying fishes, around the outside of the building. The terminal is currently used by the Delta Shuttle, and one can take a water bus from the old flying boat dock to the lower East Side of Manhattan.

PLATE 38.

Boeing B-314 **Atlantic Clipper** *at moorings in the Tagus River, opposite Lisbon waterfront, 1940*

"She has a comfortable look, like a duck planted firm and broad on the water; she doesn't seem much of a flier."

Lisbon was the European end of the more southerly North Atlantic route. From there, the Clippers flew west via the Azores, Bermuda, and on to Baltimore or New York. As Hitler's armies swamped continental Europe, and Italy joined the Axis powers, Portugal became the only friendly air route between Britain and Africa, and thence to the Middle East and the Orient. The historic and dignified city of Lisbon became a vital connection between the countries of the free world.

During the war years, Lisbon saw plenty of flying boats on the Tagus. Pan American had five Boeings in the Atlantic Division, BOAC had three, and the British also operated the Short *Golden Hind* and *Golden Horn*, together with the smaller "C" class boats. Tragically, one of the Boeing Clippers ended up in the bottom of the river bed when, in February 1943, the captain of *Yankee Clipper* misjudged his final approach and touched a wingtip into the water.

The most amazing wartime adventure was that of the *Pacific Clipper*, under the command of Captain Robert Ford. His Boeing was caught en route to Auckland, New Zealand, when the Japanese attacked Pearl Harbor, and it was deemed unwise to return via Canton Island and Honolulu. Ford headed west,

across the Tasman Sea, across Australia, the Dutch East Indies, Ceylon, Karachi, Bahrain, Khartoum, Léopoldville in the Congo, Belém in Brazil, Trinidad, and Puerto Rico to New York. It took Ford and his crew three weeks to make the journey, and they had a great deal to improvise along the way. Much of the time they had to use regular auto gasoline, not aviation spirit, and the engines suffered grievously. One engine had to be extensively rebuilt while stopping at Trincomalee, Ceylon, but the worst moment was at Léopoldville. The heavily overladen plane, tanked up to make the Atlantic crossing, had the greatest difficulty in lifting from the water. The air was still, humid, and sultry; the only help came from a six-knot current downstream. It took ninety-one seconds to get airborne from the coffee-colored water. The Boeing managed to struggle free just before the river plunged into rapids, and she labored a long time more at full power, at considerable risk of ruining the engines, before she cleared the gorges and at last began to climb.

They made it to Belém, and thence by more moderate stages home. The control tower at La Guardia heard—in disbelief—a radioed request for permission to land from "Pan American Airways' *Pacific Clipper*, out of Auckland, New Zealand."

PLATE 39.

Foynes, on the Shannon River, Ireland, 1941. Two Boeing B-314s, one Short S 23, and one Short Sunderland flying boat at moorings

When the airlines contemplated crossing the North Atlantic in 1936, they picked a point called Rineanna, on the Shannon River near Limerick, for a flying boat base. A landplane aerodrome was to be built nearby, and when it was eventually completed after the Second World War it became a well-known stop for transatlantic travelers called Shannon Airport. In the meantime, flying boat operations started a little downstream, at Foynes, a small gray town on the south bank. Foynes became the jumping-off place for transatlantic flights from northern Europe. Botwood, on the north coast of Newfoundland, was their first stop on the other side.

In 1937, Pan American and Imperial simultaneously made their first proving flights; and in 1939, a Boeing Clipper started the first scheduled passenger service on this northern route. This was closely followed by Imperial with a mail-only service, making use of flight refueling.

When the war began, the soft, rainswept landscape of County Limerick quietly became a nerve center for international air traffic. Vital wartime dispatches and important passengers passed through Foynes. Flying took place at night, and the whole operation was kept well out of the news. British and American civilian flying boats continued to operate throughout the darkest days of the war. Most of the traffic went south to Lisbon, whence connections were made to West Africa and thence to the East, or to the Azores, en route to America.

No doubt the civil aircraft movements were known to the Germans, and on one occasion a Boeing B-314 was intercepted by a Ju 87 Stuka over the Bay of Biscay. The dive bomber took up station alongside the Clipper, but its pilot did no more than slide back his cockpit cover to have a better look.

In June 1942, a Sikorsky VS-44 of American Export Airlines made the first flight direct from Foynes to New York. This was the start of a scheduled service, which took nearly twenty-six hours' flying time. The pilot was Captain Charles F. Blair, a man with a passion for flying boats. Years later, he started his own flying boat airline in the West Indies and married the wonderful Irish actress Maureen O'Hara. The Blairs retained a special association with Foynes, and with Margaret O'Shaughnessy, who has created at Foynes the world's only flying boat museum. Her boundless enthusiasm has drawn together threads from both sides of the Atlantic. Maureen O'Hara performed the opening of the museum.

PLATE 40.

Sikorsky VS-44A Excalibur, *1942*

This Vought-Sikorsky flying boat was originally designed as a Navy patrol bomber, and the experimental version flew in 1937. The Navy decided not to proceed with it. Pan American was already committed to the Boeing 314, but in 1940, American Export Airlines (AEA) ordered three civilian versions of the VS-44 for commercial service across the North Atlantic. Though smaller than the Boeing, the Sikorsky had a slightly greater range. Powered by four Pratt & Whitney Twin Wasp 1,200 hp radial engines, she had a cruising speed of 150 mph, and accommodation for up to forty-two passengers on shorter flights. She was capable, with a modest payload, of flying about 3,100 miles, just enough to permit transatlantic operation from New York to Foynes in Ireland without a refueling stop in Newfoundland. The Sikorskys were operated on this route by AEA on behalf of the Naval Air Transport Service from May 1942 until 1945. In that year, AEA was purchased by American Airlines, and the new company took the name American Overseas Airlines. The two surviving flying boats were sold to South American owners.

The three VS-44s were called *Excalibur, Excambian,* and *Exeter. Excambian* was the last to survive. She returned to the States in 1957 and was used to fly between Long Beach and Catalina Island, California, as Avalon Air Transport. Finally, Captain Charles F. Blair, ex-chief pilot of AEA, bought her. He renamed the airplane *Excalibur VII* and added her to his collection of marine aircraft operating as Antilles Air Boats out of the American Virgin Islands. This particular aircraft, now back to its old name *Excambian,* has been lovingly restored by Sikorsky volunteers and is on public display at the New England Air Museum at Bradley Field near Hartford, Connecticut. No more graceful flying boat was ever made.

PLATE 41.

Consolidated PBY-5A "Black Cat," Guadalcanal, 1943

The PBY-5A, or Catalina, as it was named by the British, was one of the most individualistic planes of World War II, and one which inspired much affection. It was built in far greater numbers than any other type of flying boat. Some 3,500 were manufactured, almost all for military use. The next most numerous was the Martin Mariner, of which 1,370 were built, and then the Short Sunderland, of which 750 were produced as military versions of the "Empire" boats.

The PBY was adopted by the US Navy as a patrol bomber in 1936, and was thus one of the oldest warplane types to see service throughout the Second World War. She was slow, but she had tremendous range and was "tough as old boots." The Catalina proved herself adaptable to new roles and to weapons that were not yet conceived when the aircraft was designed. Her dignified elegance endeared her to airmen of sixteen nations.

In the Solomons, the Marines of Squadron VP-12 found that their Cats were vulnerable to Zeros by day; but painted matte black and operating by night, they achieved striking success against enemy shipping. They were also used to great effect throughout the Pacific as air-sea rescue planes.

The PBY served during the war with honor all around the world, and until about 1965 it soldiered on in inaccessible parts such as Alaska, China, Indonesia, Chile, and the western Pacific. Many were supplied as amphibians. It was one of the few flying boat types equipped with retractable wingtip floats.

Consolidated PB2Y-2 Coronado. 115 ft wingspan, range 3,700 miles. 217 were built, used as a patrol bomber and as a transport.

Kawanishi H8K-2 Emily. 124 ft wingspan, range 4,500 miles. Assessed as having the best performance of any flying boat in the Second World War. Over 150 were built in 1942-43, of which thirty-six were employed to maintain a scheduled transport service over a wide area of the western Pacific.

PLATE 42.

Short S 25 Sunderland III taxiing for takeoff from the Cattewater, RAF Mount Batten, Plymouth, 1943

During the years of the Second World War, flying boats played a major role in the Allies' war effort. The Sunderland prototype first flew in 1937, and by the outbreak of war in September 1939, four Royal Air Force squadrons were equipped with the type. It became the longest serving aircraft in the RAF, the last examples being retired in 1959. Sunderlands operated in the Mediterranean, the Indian Ocean, the South Atlantic, and the Pacific, as well as in home waters, and they continued in service in New Zealand until 1966. The warplane proved to be a most successful maritime patrol aircraft, particularly effective in anti-submarine warfare.

The principal production model was the Mark III, seen here, which could carry a bomb load of up to 2,000 pounds, consisting of bombs, mines, or anti-submarine depth charges. Defensive armament consisted of no less than twelve machine guns. Eight were mounted in three power-operated turrets, plus a battery of four fixed guns in the nose which were used to strafe a surfaced submarine. The flying boat had a range of 2,700 miles with a bomb load of 1,700 pounds, and her top speed was 213 mph. The Sunderland was equipped with anti-surface vessel radar and with Leigh lights for submarine hunting, and German U-boat captains respectfully named her the *Stachelschwein* (porcupine).

Mount Batten RAF station was situated on a peninsula in Plymouth Sound, close to Sutton Harbour and the Citadel. It started life under the name RNAS Cattewater; this was where NC-4 arrived at the end of the very first aerial crossing of the Atlantic, in May 1919. During the Second World War, several RAF and Royal Australian Air Force squadrons, equipped with Sunderlands, were based at Mount Batten.

PLATE 43.

Boeing B-314 alighting at Bathurst, the Gambia, with President Franklin Roosevelt on board, 1943

In January 1943, two Pan American Airways Boeing Clippers were assigned to fly President Roosevelt to attend the Casablanca Conference. They conveyed the presidential party from Miami via Trinidad and Belém, Brazil, to Bathurst in the British colony of Gambia on the bulge of West Africa. From there, the last thousand miles to Morocco were covered by landplane. The cruiser USS *Memphis* was stationed in the mouth of the Gambia River to provide a communications base and overnight accommodation for the party. *Memphis* was termed the Pink Lady on account of the curious tinge of her West African camouflage scheme. The Pan American crews were accommodated on board for the duration of the conference.

John Leslie, head of the Atlantic Division of Pan American, was in charge of the flight. For security reasons, the purpose of the mission was disclosed to very few people, and he designated the two aircraft as Clippers Number One and Two. This was the origin of the convention by which the president's airplane is today called Air Force One.

Leslie, a lieutenant commander in the US Navy Reserve, reported smartly on return before the admiral in charge of the naval district. He was greeted by the phrase: "Welcome back, commodore." An officer in charge of two or more vessels is accorded the courtesy rank of commodore for the duration of his command.

Leslie had one moment of acute anxiety, when an unexpected change of the president's plans called for night takeoff. There was no chance to express concern to his superiors over the risk of encountering unlit obstructions in the busy river, and Leslie decided to take off first in Clipper Number Two. Fortunately no native fishing craft were in the way. He anxiously watched from the navigation dome until he was sure that the running lights showed that Clipper Number One was safely airborne.

PLATE 44.

Short S 25 Hythe Himalaya *overflying the Pyramids of Gizeh, Cairo, 1946*

Some clarification is necessary on the matter of names. Short S 25 Sunderland aircraft built during the Second World War for the Royal Air Force were made available for civilian use. The British Overseas Airways Corporation, successor to Imperial Airways, operated about thirty Sunderland IIIs during the war years as civilian transports, and after the war twenty-two of these planes were upgraded by the airline at its maintenance base in Hythe. These converted warplanes were consequently named Hythes.

The aircraft manufacturers, Short Brothers, took in hand twenty-one ex-RAF Sunderland Vs and gave them more radical modifications to suit civilian use. These were described as Short S 25 Sandringhams. Nine were sold to airlines in Argentina and New Zealand, and twelve went to BOAC. To add to the confusion, the airline called nine of these the Plymouth class and the remaining three, a slightly different variant, were called Bermudas.

In the picture we see a Short Hythe named *Himalaya* circuiting the pyramids before landing on the Nile at Rod-El-Farag, on the right bank just north of the center of Cairo.

Short Shetland. 150 ft wingspan, range 4,400 miles. Two were built in 1944-47, but they were not adopted for military or civilian use.

PLATE 45.

Latécoère 631 at Martinique, 1947

One of the last of the large commercial flying boats was this French airplane that went into airline service in 1947. She came too late, for by then landplanes were available with the necessary range and reliability to cross the ocean, and their economics were far superior. No longer were airlines constrained by the need to provide their own landing fields, and so they soon gave up using flying boats and reequipped with landplane types.

The Laté 631, for which an order was placed in 1938, was originally to be powered by six Gnome-Rhône engines of a projected power of 1,650 hp. They never materialized. The first production version in 1946 was equipped with Wright Cyclone twin-row radial engines of similar power, and they gave the airplane an impressive performance. Her load-to-tare ratio was 55 : 45, her cruising speed 185 mph, and her operating range was claimed to be 3,700 miles. She had slender, tapered wings, horizontal stabilizers with marked dihedral, and twin tail fins. Retractable floats were mounted in the outboard engine nacelles.

Dornier Do 24 V-4, some of which were used by the Dutch Navy

Had the Second World War not erupted in 1939, the Laté 631 might easily have challenged, for a few years at least, the Boeing B-314 for the aerial Blue Riband of the Atlantic. She would have been a fitting successor to the *Normandie.*

PLATE 46.

Latécoère 631 flying over Fort-de-France, Martinique, 1947

The biggest flying boat ever to go into airline service, the six-engined Laté 631, was also the most stylish. Her rakish exterior was matched by the most sumptuous Modern Movement interior, sporting a bar counter with stools and a restaurant with chromium-plated leather-cushioned chairs. There were fourteen two-berth cabins and four with four berths, for a total accommodation of forty-four.

Intended for introduction on the North Atlantic route from France to North America, development and production were stalled in 1940 by the war and German occupation of northern France. Work on the flying boat continued nevertheless, at a slow pace, in Toulouse, located in the southern part of the country which remained under Vichy control. The prototype eventually flew in November 1942. After that, the German military authorities stopped all further work. Immediately after the war the second production plane was completed and it was sent on a demonstration flight to Argentina. At this stage, the French aircraft industry was subjected to nationalization and further production was delayed. In due course, ten examples of the Laté 631 were built, of which four were delivered to the national airline Air France.

In July 1947, the airline started a scheduled service from Biscarosse, near Bordeaux, to Port Etienne (400 miles north of Dakar), and thence to Fort-de-France in Martinique. During the war the evolution of aircraft types and of aero engines had been accelerated, and landplanes now had the capability of flying the Atlantic. The flying boat operation could not compete economically, and it was brought to an end in less than a year.

Restaurant in a Laté 631, with chromium-plated tubular steel and leather furniture à la mode *Le Corbusier*

PLATE 47.

*Short S 45 Solent **Salisbury** overflying the Victoria Falls before landing on the Zambezi River, 1949*

It was a Wagnerian setting for a landing. From May 1948, Short Solents of BOAC alighted on the Zambezi, immediately upstream from the crashing cascade of Victoria Falls. When the river is in spate, a plume of spray hangs like a curtain above the mile-wide stream, rising a thousand feet into the air. Before reaching the falls, the river flows between low banks and scattered islands which are loaded with tropical growth. The flying boats came down between Canary and Livingstone Islands, and passengers came ashore at the Livingstone Boat Club, or, on the southern side, to a boathouse just above the falls, from which point they took a bus to the Victoria Falls Hotel.

Downstream, the Zambezi drops nearly 400 feet into a dark, narrow canyon that twists and turns as the river gouges its way eastwards through the plateau. The hotel is sited downriver, looking upstream from the first turn of the gorge towards the curtain of spray. The falls are visible through the arch of a spindly steel lattice bridge which links Zimbabwe to Zambia (at that time, Southern and Northern Rhodesia). The railway bridge, said Cecil Rhodes, should be built so close to the falls that carriage windows would be wetted by the spray.

The hotel is a period piece, built by the railway company when the line reached the Zambezi at the beginning of the last century. It is a sprawling Edwardian country house with generous passages and spacious rooms. A central axis comprises a gracious sequence of courtyards, loggias, and terraces which glide out into a park-like landscape, shaded by magnificent spreading trees. Proceeding through the building, visitors walk out into the gardens, which descend by a series of gentle downward stages towards the incessant thunder of the distant falls.

The landing place at Victoria Falls came into use when longer-range flying boats were available to take over from the old S 23 "Empire" boats, which had followed a route down the east coast of Africa. From 1948 to 1950, Short Solents operated what was called the "Springbok Service" to South Africa. Between Port Bell, on Lake Victoria near Kampala, and Vaaldam, near Johannesburg, they made a single stop, at Victoria Falls, to serve passengers destined for the Rhodesias. Occasional flights diverted instead to Cape Maclear, on Lake Nyasa, to serve Nyasaland-bound passengers.

PLATE 48.

Short S 45 Solent Mk IV Aotearoa *landing at Waitemata Harbour, Auckland, 1950*

Aotearoa was the name given to New Zealand's first Short S 23 "Empire" flying boat, which landed at Waitemata Harbour in August 1939. She was joined by her sister ship *Awarua* in the service of Tasman Empire Airways Ltd. Immediately after the war, the "Empire" boats were replaced on the 1,200-mile service across the Tasman Sea to Australia by four Short S 25 Sandringhams. These ex-RAF Sunderland aircraft proved to be unequal to the crossing, and five Short S 45 Solents were ordered in 1949 to supersede them. The first to arrive, again named *Aotearoa*, was soon joined by *Ararangi*, *Awatere*, *Aranui*, and *Arapina*, which operated not only between Wellington and Auckland to Sydney, but also on services to the Chatham Islands, Fiji, the Cook Islands, Tahiti, Western Samoa, and Tonga. The Solents were withdrawn in September 1960.

Waitemata Harbour lies on the north side of the isthmus on which the city of Auckland is located, in the North Island of New Zealand. Note the New Zealand national flag painted on the Solent's tail fin. It portrays the Southern Cross in red stars, each outlined in white, on a dark blue background. The aircraft is flying New Zealand's version of the Civil Air Ensign, surmounting the Royal Air Mail Pennant on the starboard flagstaff, together with the national flag to port.

The crew of the first Pan American flying boat to arrive in New Zealand, a Sikorsky S-42 in March 1937, experienced some anxiety in making a landfall after their long flight from Samoa, navigating by dead reckoning. John Leslie, then chief engineer of the Pacific Division, first detected the presence of land when he spied what looked like "a long white cloud" on the horizon. Once they were safely on the ground he described this experience to his hosts and was met with astonishment. "In Maori we speak of our country as *Aotearoa*," he was told by the mayor of Auckland. "Literally, this means a *long white cloud*."

PLATE 49.

Short S 45 Solent II Somerset *at Cape Maclear, Lake Nyasa, November 1950*

The last flight of a BOAC flying boat in scheduled service took place in November 1950, when RMA *Somerset* flew from Southampton to Vaaldam, an artificial lake formed by a dam on the Vaal River some seventy miles from Johannesburg. On the return journey, the aircraft landed at Cape Maclear on Lake Nyasa, Nyasaland (now Malawi).

Cape Maclear was an overnight stop. It is a lovely spot. Passengers and crew stayed at a resort hotel built on the site of the old Livingstonia Mission. The Cape lies at the southern end of what is now called Lake Malawi, a place of special scenic beauty in a country which has some of the finest scenery in Africa. The flying boats moored at Otter Point, which can be seen in the picture, at the southern end of a magnificent bay which is sheltered on the lake side by three islands.

The cape was named by Dr. David Livingstone, who, with Dr. John Kirk, found it during an exploratory expedition up the Shire River in 1861. He particularly mentions "a grand, old, sacred fig tree whose wide-spreading branches threw their kindly shade over the burial-ground." This enormous tree can still be identified, along with several other splendid specimens. Livingstone died in 1873 in what is now Zambia, and two years later the Livingstonia Mission was established by Dr. Robert Laws at Cape Maclear on behalf of the Free Church of Scotland in Edinburgh. The Scots Kirk missionaries here and throughout Nyasaland have made a great and lasting impression

BOAC stepped bus, for passengers with their baggage underneath

on the indigenous culture. Dr. Kirk went from Nyasaland to become a long-time British consul in Zanzibar, the confidant and guide to successive sultans.

The Solent was a civilian version of the Short Seaford, a wartime development of the Sunderland. The Seaford came too late to see service in the war, but the civilian airliner was years in advance of the old "Empire" boats which she resembled. The Solents used by BOAC had a range of 2,400 miles, a speed of 230 mph and seats for thirty to forty passengers. A rather unusual feature of the interior was a ship's library.

PLATE 50.

Saunders-Roe SR 45 Princess flying boats near Calshot Castle, Southampton Water, 1952

Three Princess flying boats were built, but only one was completed and flew, so this painting shows a scene that never took place. She was such an elegant airplane, however, that I wanted to give as complete a picture of her as possible. I saw the SR 45 fly past at the Farnborough Air Show in 1957, skimming just a few feet above the concrete runway. She looked unbelievably huge, and she was mysteriously quiet.

The SR 45 was designed during the war years, and the three aircraft were ordered in 1946 to meet a BOAC requirement for a transatlantic flying boat to operate directly from Southampton to New York with more than 100 passenger seats. The hull was a deep figure eight in section, like the fuselage of the Boeing B-377 Stratocruiser, and she was the only pressurized flying boat passenger airplane ever built. The Princess was an enormous aircraft, with two freight holds on the lower deck, two refreshment bars, and a galley, in addition to passenger seating on the upper deck. The military version was to have been capable of carrying two hundred troops.

Power was intended to be provided by twelve Rolls-Royce Tweed turbo-prop engines in six nacelles, the motors coupled together driving contra-rotating propellers. The Tweed engine project was canceled, and the Princess was powered instead by ten Bristol Proteus turboprops. This engine initially fell short of providing the thrust it was designed for, and the coupled gearing arrangement proved troublesome in development. The first Princess flew in 1952, but completion of the second and third examples was delayed pending development of the 3,650 hp Proteus 705 engine.

By 1951, BOAC had decided to go for a fleet of all landplane aircraft, and the Princess was thereafter earmarked as a military transport. The three prototypes were cocooned and laid up at the Royal Air Force station at Calshot Castle for many years. This is situated on a prominent sandspit at the entrance to Southampton Water, close to the path of the great transatlantic liners, rails lined with passengers, as they made their way up towards Southampton. In the 1930s, the big J-class racing yachts such as *Velsheda, Endeavour II,* and *Shamrock V* would often have been seen sailing in the vicinity of Calshot, particularly during July about the time of Cowes Week.

PLATE 51.

Grumman G-38 Goose of Antilles Airboats at Saint Thomas, 1973

Charlie Blair, chief pilot of American Export Airlines, later flew for Pan American Airways. In 1967, he started an airline in the US Virgin Islands called Antilles Airboats. Blair was a great flying boat enthusiast; his airline's fleet included twenty Grumman Gooses, several Mallards, two Short Sandringhams, and one Sikorsky VS-44A aircraft. Airline parlance differed from ornithology.

Between 1937 and 1945, 345 Grumman Gooses were built, all of them amphibians, mostly for the Navy and Coast Guard. The sturdy little twin-engined flying boat was a versatile airplane, and many examples remained in commercial service, particularly in Alaska and in the Caribbean, until recent years.

The two big fat Pratt & Whitney R-985 radial engines seemed to dwarf the airplane, which generally had the capacity for six passengers in addition to a crew of two.

Blohm & Voss BV 238. 200 ft wingspan, never entered service before the end of the war.

Dornier Do J Wal of Japan Airlines

PLATE 52.

Grumman G-73 Turbo Mallard of Virgin Islands
Seaplane Shuttle at Saint Thomas, 1986

The Mallard was an enlarged version of the Goose. She was a ten-passenger amphibian, fifty-nine of which were built between 1946 and 1951. An even larger variant, called the JR2F Albatross, was built in numbers for the US Navy and Coast Guard.

Twelve Mallards were converted to Turbo Mallards by replacing their Pratt & Whitney piston engines with PT6-34 turboprop engines manufactured by the Canadian division of the same company. The new engines produced twice the power with half the weight of the reciprocating type, and time between overhauls was increased from 450 hours to 1,500 hours (or 3,000 hours for many procedures). Passenger capacity was increased to seventeen.

With their retractable wheeled undercarriages, the amphibians' operations were far quicker and easier as they could taxi straight up a ramp and out of the water for passenger disembarkation and for maintenance. On at least one occasion, a heavy landing caused a serious rupture in the hull, but the Mallard was able to scramble up onto dry land just in time to avoid foundering.

The Mallards remained in service with Virgin Islands Seaplane Shuttle between Saint Croix, Saint Thomas, Tortola, and Saint John until 1989.

Martin Mars. 200 ft wingspan, 30,000 lb of cargo, range 4,600 miles. One example saw war service; later she was joined in the US Navy by five sister ships.

BIBLIOGRAPHY

Allward, Maurice. *Seaplanes and Flying Boats.* Ashbourne, UK: Moorland Publishing Co, 1981.

Beatty, David. *The Water Jump.* London: Secker & Warburg, 1976.

Brock, Horace. *Flying the Oceans.* New York: Jason Aronson, 1978.

Cobham, Sir Alan. *Twenty Thousand Miles in a Flying Boat.* London: George Harrap & Co, 1930.

Cochrane, Hardesty, & Lee. *The Aviation Careers of Igor Sikorsky.* Seattle, WA: U of Washington Press, 1989.

Cohen, Stan. *Wings to the Orient.* Missoula, MT: Pictorial Histories Publishing Co, 1985.

Cole-King. *Cape Maclear.* Zomba, Malawi: Malawi Government Dept. of Antiquities, 1968.

La Conquête de l'Atlantique Nord. ICARE (Revue Francaise), 4 vols.

Conrad, Barnaby III. *Pan Am: An Aviation Legend.* Emeryville, CA: Woodford Press, 1999.

Coster, Graham. *Corsairville.* London: Viking, 2000.

Crouch, Tom. *The Bishop's Boys: A Life of Wilbur & Orville Wright.* New York: W.W. Norton & Co, 1989.

Daley, Robert. *An American Saga.* New York: Random House, 1980.

Davies, R. E. G. *Lufthansa: An Airline and its Aircraft.* McLean, VA: Paladwr Press, 1991.

———. *Pan Am: An Airline and its Aircraft.* New York: Orion Books, 1987.

Davis, Peter J. *East African—An Airline Story.* Egham, UK: Runnymede Malthouse, 1993.

Dornier: A brief history of the company. Friedrichshafen, Germany: 1983.

Durrell, Gerald. *My Family and Other Animals.* Harmondsworth, UK: Penguin Books, 1959.

Frater, Alexander. *Beyond the Blue Horizon.* London: William Heinemann, 1986.

Gandt, Robert. *China Clipper.* Annapolis, MD: US Naval Institute Press, 1991.

Grey, C. G. *Sea-Flyers.* London: Faber & Faber, 1942.

Harrison, Lockstone, & Anderson. *The Golden Age of New Zealand Flying Boats.* New Zealand: Random House, 1997.

Hodgkinson, Nic. *Beachcomber—The Story of a Sandringham.* Southampton, UK: 1992.

Jablonsky, Edward. *Sea Wings.* New York: Doubleday & Co, 1972.

Jackson, A. S. *Imperial Airways.* London: Terence Dalton, 1990.

Klaás, M. D. *The Last of the Flying Clippers.* Atglen, PA: Schiffer, 1997.

Knott Richard. *The American Flying Boat.* Annapolis, MD: US Naval Institute Press, 1979.

Krupnick, John E. *Pacific Pioneers.* Missoula, MT: Pictorial Histories Publishing Co, 1997.

Levering, Robert. *The Clipper Heritage.* Inter-Collegiate Press for Airline Pilots' Association of PAA, 1984.

Lowe, David. *The Flying Boat Era.* Auckland, New Zealand: Lodestar Press.

Mayborn, Mitch et al. *The Grumman Guidebook.* Dallas, TX: Flying Enterprise Publications, 1976.

Mondey, David. *British Aircraft of World War II.* Feltham, UK: Temple Press, 1982.

Munson, Kenneth. *Flying Boats and Seaplanes.* New York: Macmillan Co, 1971.

Nicolaou, Stéphane. *Flying Boats and Seaplanes.* Osceola, WI: MBI Publishing Co, 1998.

Pomeroy, Colin. *The Flying Boats of Bermuda.* Dorchester, UK: 2000.

Taylor, Sir Gordon. *The Sky Beyond.* New York: Bantam Books.

Teague, Dennis C. *Mount Batten: Flying Boat Base, Plymouth.* Plymouth, UK: Westway, 1986.

Thomas, Don. *Nostalgia Panamericana.* 1987

Trippe, Betty Stettinius. *Pan Am's First Lady.* McLean, VA: Paladwr Press, 1996.

Yenne, Bill. *Seaplanes of the World.* Cobb, CA: O.G. Publishing Inc., 1997.

Imperial Airways Heracles-*class landplane of 1931*

INDEX

Index does not include place-names.

Aeromarine Airways, 32
Aeropostale, 56
Air France, 21, 27, 50, 56, 92, 120
Alcock and Brown, 16
Aldrich (see Delano and Aldrich)
Algérie, 50
America, 30
American Airlines, 108
American Clipper, 42
American Export Airlines (AEA), 28, 106, 108, 130
American Overseas Airlines, 108
Antilles Air Boats, 28, 108, 130
Antilles Clipper, 78
Aotearoa, 124
Aranui, 124
Arapina, 124
Ararangi, 124
Archbold, Richard, 92
Armstrong-Siddeley, 6, 70
Athlone Castle, 60
Atlantic Clipper, 104
Avalon Air Transport, 108
Awarua, 124
Awatere, 124
Baby Clipper (see Sikorsky S-43)
Bahamasair, 92
Bermuda Clipper, 84
Berwick, 27
Betsy (see Sikorsky S-42)
Biltmore Hotel, Miami, 46
Blackburn Iris, 50
Blair, Charles F., 106, 108, 130
Blériot 5190, 21, 56
Blohm & Voss BV 222, 7, 22
Blohm & Voss BV 238, 130
Blohm & Voss Ha 139, 22, 72
Boeing 314 (see Boeing B-314)
Boeing 747, 19
Boeing B-15, 26
Boeing B-17, 26
Boeing B-314, 15, 17, 25, 26, 27, 28, 90, 96, 102, 104, 106, 114, 118
Boeing B-377 Stratocruiser, 128
Boeing Clippers, 13, 15, 17, 26, 68, 90, 96, 102, 104, 106, 114
Borger, John, 78
Bouilloux-Lafont, Marcel, 56
Bréguet 530 Saigon, 50
Bréguet Bizerte, 50

Bréguet Dakar, 50
Bristol (engines), 20, 40, 82, 128
British India Line, 82
British Overseas Airways Corporation (BOAC), 28, 104, 116, 122, 126, 128
British Power Boat Company, 82, 94
Burgess, W. Starling, 30
Cabot, 100
Calpurnia, 24
Calypso, 82
Camilla, 80
Canadian Pacific, 100
Canopus, 24
Capella, 70, 80
Capricornus, 24
Caribbean Clipper, 42
Caribou, 100
Carnauba, 52
Casa Marina Hotel, 32
Casablanca Conference, 27, 114
Cassiopeia, 24, 88
Cathay Pacific, 92
Cavalier, 84
Ceres, 94
Chennault's Flying Tigers, 27
China Clipper, 2, 54, 66, 86
Churchill, Winston, 27
City of Alexandria, *City of Athens*, et. al., 60
Clippers (see Boeing Clippers)
Cobham, Sir Alan, 24, 34, 60
Columbus, 32
Consolidated B-24 Liberator, 25
Consolidated Commodore, 15, 38, 46
Consolidated P2Y-3, 50
Consolidated PB2Y-2 Coronado, 28, 110
Consolidated PBY Catalina, 15, 27, 92, 110
Consolidated XP2Y-1, 38
Copacabana Palace Hotel, 38
Coriolanus, 24, 80
Croix du Sud, 21, 44, 56
Curtiss F-5L, 30, 32
Curtiss H-12, 30
Curtiss H-16, 30
Curtiss NC-1 to NC-4, 16, 30, 112
Curtiss, Glenn, 30
de Havilland Albatross, 25
de Havilland Mosquito, 25

Delano and Aldrich, 102
Deutsche Lufthansa, 22, 74
Dixie Clipper, 96
Dornier Do 18, 22, 72
Dornier Do 24, 22, 118
Dornier Do 26, 22, 74
Dornier Do J Wal, 22, 50, 74, 130
Dornier Do X, 21, 72
Dornier Super Wal, 74
Douglas DC-2, 58, 66
Douglas DC-4 (C-54), 28, 78
Douglas PD-1, 50
Durrell, Gerald, 36
Empress of Australia, 100
Endeavour II, 128
Excalibur, 108
Excambian, 108
Exeter, 108
Flagler, Henry, 32
Focke-Wulf Fw 200 Condor, 22
Ford Tri-Motor, 38, 42
Ford, Robert, 104
Franco, General, 27
Friesenland, 74
Gnome-Rhône (engines), 118
Golden Gate International Exposition, 90
Golden Hind, 25, 104
Golden Horn, 104
Graf Zeppelin, 21
Gronau, Wolfgang von, 74
Grumman G-38 Goose, 28, 130, 132
Grumman G-73 Turbo Mallard, 132
Grumman JR2F Albatross, 132
Grumman Mallard, 28, 130, 132
Guba, 92
Handley Page 42, 22, 24
Hawaiian Clipper, 66
Hearst, William Randolph, 46
Heathrow Airport, 100
Heracles, 22, 24, 134
Highball Express, 32
Himalaya, 116
Hindenburg, 21, 24
Hispano-Suiza, 6, 50, 56, 98
Hitler, Adolf, 17, 104
Honolulu Clipper, 90
Hoover, Mrs. Herbert, 42

Horseshoe Route, 27
Hughes H-4 *Spruce Goose*, 28
Hughes, Howard, 28
Hunting Clan Viscount, 64
Hurricane Hugo, 28
Ile de France, 21
Imperial Airways, 6, 19, 22, 24-27, 36, 40, 46, 60, 64, 76, 80, 82, 84, 88, 94, 100, 106, 116
Jamaica Clipper, 58
Johnson, Herbert F., 52
Johnson, Martin and Osa, 52
Junkers Jumo, 72
Junkers Ju 87 Stuka, 106
Kaiser, Henry J., 28
Kawanishi H8K Emily, 110
King George V, 100
Kirk, John, 126
KLM (Dutch airline), 92
La Guardia Airport, 26, 102, 104
Latécoère 28, 56
Latécoère 300, 21, 22, 44, 56
Latécoère 521, 21, 98
Latécoère 522, 98
Latécoère 581, 12, 98
Latécoère 631, 21, 118, 120
Laws, Robert, 126
Leslie, John, 5, 19, 20, 114, 124
Leuteritz, Hugo, 19
Liberty engines, 30
Lieutenant de Vaisseau Paris, 98
Lindbergh, Charles, 16, 19
Lindsey, Lou, 78
Livingstone, David, 126
Lockheed 14 Super Electra, 25
Lockheed Constellation, 28, 78
Lockheed Hudson, 25
Lodeesen, Marius, 13, 54
Lufthansa (see Deutsche Lufthansa)
Luftwaffe, 7, 22
Lurline, 90
Maia, 76
Manchester, 92
Manila Hotel, 86
Mariposa, 90
Martin M-130, 2, 20-22, 25, 26, 54, 66, 86
Martin Mars, 28, 132
Martin PBM-3 Mariner, 28, 110
Martin PM-1, 50
Martin, Glenn, 26
Matson Line, 90
Mayflower, 64
Mayo, Major, 76
Memphis, 114
Mercury, 24, 76

Mermoz, Jean, 56
Merrick, George, 46
Model 75 Aeromarine Cruiser, 32
Monterey, 90
Musick, Edwin C., 19, 54, 68, 86
Mussolini, Benito, 40
Napier Sabre, 20
Navy Curtiss, 16, 30
New York, Rio, and Buenos Aires Line (NYRBA), 15, 38, 46, 52
Nordmeer, 72
Nordstern, 72
Nordwind, 72
Normandie, 21, 98, 118
O'Hara, Maureen, 106
O'Neill, Ralph, 38
O'Shaughnessy, Margaret, 106
Ostmark, 74
P & O Steamship Company, 24
Pacific Clipper, 27, 104
Pan American Airways, 5, 13, 15, 17, 19, 20, 22, 24, 25, 26, 28, 38, 42, 44, 46, 48, 52, 54, 58, 62, 66, 68, 78, 80, 84, 90, 96, 102, 104, 106, 108, 114, 124, 130
Pan American-Grace Airways (Panagra), 52, 62
Panair do Brasil, 17, 52, 62
Philippine Clipper, 66, 86
Pierce Arrow (automobiles), 42
Porte, John, 30, 76
Pratt and Whitney (engines), 19, 22, 38, 46, 48, 62, 86, 90, 108, 130, 132
Priester, André, 5, 13, 19, 25, 68, 80
Qantas, 80, 92
Queen Mary, 100
Queen Victoria, 46
Quezon, Manuel, 54
R34 (airship), 16
Read, Lt. Commander, 16
Red Top Cab Co., 48
Rhodes, Cecil, 122
Rolls-Royce (engines), 20, 128
Roosevelt, Franklin D., 27, 54, 114
Royal Aeronautical Society, 27
Samoan Clipper, 68
Santos Dumont, 21, 56
Santos Dumont Airport, 58, 62
Sao Paulo, 62
Satyrus, 22, 60
Saunders-Roe SR 45 Princess, 128
Savoia-Marchetti S.55, 34
Schwabenland, 72, 74
Scipio, 22, 40, 60
Scott-Paine, Hubert, 82
Servicio Aereo Condor, 27
Shamrock V, 128
Short Bermuda, 116

Short F-5 Felixstowe, 30
Short S 8 Calcutta, 36, 60
Short S 17 Kent, 22, 24, 40, 50, 60
Short S 21, 76
Short S 23, 24, 60, 64, 70, 80, 82, 84, 88, 94, 100, 106, 122, 124
Short S 25 Hythe, 116
Short S 25 Sandringham, 116, 124, 130
Short S 25 Sunderland, 27, 28, 106, 110, 112, 116, 124
Short S 26 (G-class), 25, 80
Short S 30, 82, 100
Short S 45 Solent, 28, 122, 124, 126
Short Seaford, 126
Short Shetland, 116
Short Singapore 1, 34, 50, 60
Short Brothers, 36, 116
Short-Mayo S 20, 76
Sikorsky S-38, 10, 15, 38, 42, 48, 52
Sikorsky S-40, 13, 15, 42, 48
Sikorsky S-42, 20, 48, 54, 58, 62, 66, 68, 78, 80, 84, 102, 124
Sikorsky S-43, 62
Sikorsky VS-44 (see Vought-Sikorsky)
Sikorsky, Igor, 19, 26
Somerset, 126
South-Western Hotel, Southampton, 46
Spenceley, Henry, 96
Springbok Service, 122
Stephanides, Theodore, 36
Supermarine Stranraer, 50
Sylvanus, 22, 60
Tasman Empire Airways Ltd. (TEAL), 80, 124
Taylor, Sir Gordon, 92
Thai Airways, 92
Tilton, John, 54
Trans-Australian (TAA), 92
Treasure Island Marine Air Terminal, 86
Trippe, Betty, 96
Trippe, Juan, 17, 19, 24, 25, 27, 38, 42, 54, 96
Tunisie, 50
Union Castle Line, 24, 60
Uppercu, Inglis, 32
Velsheda, 128
Vickers Vimy, 16
Victoria Air Terminal, 100
Victoria Falls Hotel, 122
Ville de Saint Pierre, 98
Virgin Islands Seaplane Shuttle, 132
Vought-Sikorsky VS-44, 28, 106, 108, 130
Wanamaker, Rodman, 30
Westfallen, 74
Winter Palace Hotel, Aswan, 88
Wright (engines), 19, 26, 90, 118
Wright brothers, 54
Yankee Clipper, 26, 104